V I P E R

Paula Jeffery

Harefield Press

Viper

Paula Jeffery

Published by: Harefield Press

Text Design: Paula Jeffery

Cover Design: Paula Jeffery

ISBN-13: 978-1-9998087-2-3

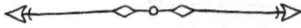

This was much harder to write than I had imagined. Narcissism is insidious by nature and sometimes so subtle that it's difficult to translate into words.

I am so grateful for all the support I've received particularly from Esther Jones, Janet Kidner, Lynne Dady and Cheryl Flynn, my beta readers who helped correct everything from clumsy to commas.

To my patient, tolerant, family, particularly Graham, because narcissism has been a major topic of conversation, pretty much constantly, for the past couple of years.

To those warriors of the internet who have opened the channels of communication in order to educate; providing countless hours of discussion and insight.

A special mention to Dana Morningstar, star of video and podcast; educator and author. At my lowest point, I watched her videos on a loop. Thank you.

Lastly and yes, least, to the cluster B's in my life, both past and present who provided me with the inspiration and determination to document this dysfunction.

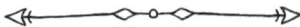

CONTENTS

INTRODUCTION

LEARNING THE LANGUAGE

SOCIAL MEDIA

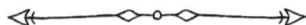

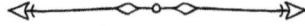

The Farmer and the Viper[*]

This story concerns a farmer who finds a viper freezing in the snow. Taking pity on it, he picks it up and places it within his coat. The viper, revived by the warmth, bites his rescuer, who dies realising that it is his own fault.

The story is recorded in both Greek and Latin sources. In the former, the farmer dies reproaching himself "for pitying a scoundrel," while in the version by Phaedrus the snake says that he bit his benefactor "to teach the lesson not to expect a reward from the wicked."

---

[*] "The Farmer and the Viper," Wikipedia, The Free Encyclopedia, https://en.wikipedia.org/w/index.php?title=The_Farmer_and_the_Viper&oldid=851340130

INTRODUCTION

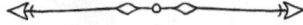

Narcissism, the buzz word of the twenty teens. Mainstream media overuses and misappropriates the term, encouraging us to use it to describe almost anyone we don't like. Selfish? You're a narcissist. Take too many selfies? You're a narcissist.

To be clear from the outset, narcissism is a continuum. We all have narcissistic traits and most of us travel that spectrum like an elevator in a skyscraper. Depending on how our life or day is going we may find ourselves on level 2 or level 20. This is not what this book is about. The people who have provided the material for my research live at the pathological end of that continuum. They never venture below level 40 and their preference is for sipping cocktails on the roof garden.

Normal narcissism is centred on a healthy, positive self image, developed from childhood and based on a regard for our own achievements and abilities. With this as a base we are able to maintain a balanced level of self respect that can shrug off the bumps and setbacks of life. In contrast the narcissism of the roof garden variety uses a shield to protect feelings of insecurity and a wounded sense of self. The pathological narcissist covers their inferiority with a veneer of entitlement and superiority, a veneer so delicate that it can be damaged by the slightest criticism whether real or imagined. The hyper-vigilant and hypersensitive narcissist struggles to conceal their inner feelings of inferiority. Any disagreement or challenge to their authority will see them lashing out and ultimately devaluing and discarding people around them, even close friends and family.

The advice often offered to those who have been in any kind of relationship with a narcissist is to NEVER share your experiences with anyone who has not suffered this type of abuse personally. You will struggle to communicate what has happened to you and worse you may present as being overly emotional, adversarial or simply a liar. This is the double whammy of a relationship with a narcissist; the abuse itself and the difficulty sharing your experience with others. There are times, when you're dealing with or are in the aftermath of a narcissistic relationship that you may question yourself. Is this even a thing? Am I imagining or exaggerating it? What if they are not a narcissist? Maybe I'm a narcissist? If you've spent any time reading through narcissistic abuse support forums online you will realise that this is a common reaction. The confusion is part of the typical fallout from this type of crazy making relationship.

Reading the experiences of narcissist's victims I was surprised that, in many cases, there appeared to be no real story. Indeed, some of the posts look confused, vindictive and petty. I have attempted several times to write about my own encounters and I liken it to knitting jelly. It is almost impossible to get to grips with covert narcissistic abuse unless the abuser is exposed in something dramatic, like living a double life. The more common, day to day, drip, drip of psychological abuse that undermines self esteem and often occurs within families over many decades can be difficult to identify when you're in the middle of it and even more difficult to communicate.

So why am I even bothering? Experiencing narcissism in my own life was a revelation that was devastating on many levels. However, I gained comfort and strength by educating myself. I read everything I could find and quickly realised that I wasn't alone. Sadly, this is nowhere near a unique experience. The more we can inform ourselves and more importantly, educate our children, the earlier we can identify problematic behaviour and avoid the inevitable pain involved in a relationship with a narcissist. Although there are many books and articles about narcissism, my feeling is the more that is written about the many different types of narcissistic relationships the more likely we are to find something that echoes our own experience. That recognition can be the catalyst to moving forward and healing.

A viper in the bosom

There is much written about the narcissist and romantic relationships, for example, how to avoid dating a narcissist and what to do if you find yourself partnered with one. This is really important and supportive information for those who find themselves in what can ultimately turn out to be a frightening situation. Although I did recognise narcissistic behaviours in past romantic affairs, the most problematic relationships I have experienced are those that I have seen played out between friends and family members and for that reason this book focusses on the covert narcissist in non-romantic relationships.

Disclaimer

I'm not an expert, I'm not a mental health professional and I don't hold any medical qualifications. The content of this book is based largely on my opinions, experiences of several emotionally abusive relationships and research gathered over several years as well as talking with others about their dealings with narcissists. As such, this book cannot be treated as 'expert' advice.

The revelation that a friend or family member is suffering from a personality disorder can be a source of distress. You know when a serial killer is arrested and the neighbours are so shocked because "...they were such a lovely person who adored their dog." Discovering narcissism can be a similar sort of revelation. This book is largely based on my own opinions and experiences. Other experiences are available and may differ.

It's worth mentioning, at this point, that if you feel in any danger of violence from a narcissist you need to get help immediately. Please do not put yourself in jeopardy by confronting a person who may respond violently. Narcissists can react unpredictably if they think the game is up and they may be about to be unmasked. People have been murdered for less, so please keep safe and contact the authorities if you believe you are in danger.

Words

For the purpose of this book, I use either gender neutral pronouns or 'he' for simplicity. However, narcissism is an equal opportunities disorder and of course there are many narcissistic women, just as there are men who are victims of narcissists.

I reluctantly use the word 'victim' throughout to describe the person who has been traumatised and abused by a narcissist. I resisted the term initially because of the weight given to it and how we see ourselves and are perceived when we are labelled in this way. However, when I used alternatives to describe the person who has suffered narcissist abuse they seemed clumsy so I'm sticking with victim, for the sake of clarity and brevity.

Crazy-making is a term often used in descriptions of the sort of underhand behaviour employed by narcissists to manipulate and confuse. I'm very aware of stigmatising the mentally ill and although I'm not entirely comfortable using the word 'crazy' in this way, I struggled to come up with an alternative that didn't read as contrived. Apologies if you find these words offensive.

DEFINITION

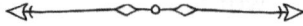

B efore listing the characteristics associated with narcissism it's important to point out that one of the traits associated with the disorder, in particular the cloaked and hidden form of narcissism, is sly and underhand dishonesty. Combine that with the type of narcissist who believes they are intellectually superior and we have an intelligent but untrustworthy person.

If such an individual gets even a hint that they are being accused of narcissism they will not just passively deny it, they will be proving, beyond all doubt that they couldn't possibly be a narcissist. They will research and present articles to support their argument. They will scour the internet and cherry pick sections of academic studies.

"See, I don't do this so I'm definitely not a narcissist."

They will take part in online tests to determine how high they are on the narcissistic scale and are likely to get a low score. Why? Because they lie. If their aim is to prove they are not a narcissist they will determine which of the test answers will score the lowest and then present you with the result. They will insist that this outcome demonstrates that, in fact, they are the opposite of a narcissist and it's likely that you, the accuser, are the real narcissist. It's worth bearing in mind the determination of a narcissist never to acknowledge their own behaviour, and the lengths they will go to in order to prove that they are not a narcissist, before we even breathe the word in their presence.

Types of Personality Disorder

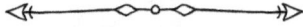

There are several types of problematic behaviour that are defined as disorders which can potentially lead to treatment and they are broadly grouped into three distinct categories; A, B & C as listed in the definitive catalogue of mental disorders, the American Psychiatric Association's DSM*.

Cluster A personality disorders are those where the person has difficulty relating to other people and their behaviour would be regarded by most people as 'not normal' or eccentric.

People with Cluster B personality disorders also have difficulty relating to other people and may display behaviour that is disturbing, dramatic or erratic. Types of Cluster B personality disorders include;

- Anti-social personality disorder (previously referred to as psychopaths and sociopaths)
- Borderline personality disorder
- Histrionic personality disorder
- Narcissistic personality disorder

---

* American Psychiatric Association. https://www.psychiatry.org. Accessed 12 June 2018.

Cluster C personality disorders are those where the sufferer fears personal relationships.

Of the four types of Cluster B, this book deals primarily with the traits and behaviours associated with Narcissistic Personality Disorder. However there are no hard lines between each type of disorder and often there is a crossover of characteristics.

Some of the signs of a narcissistic personality disorder include:

- A belief that they are special, which makes them different and more deserving than other people. They exaggerate their achievements and talents.

- They only feel worthy if others recognise their value and needs. Their fragile self-esteem depends on outside validation and they demand admiration.

- They lack empathy and are unable to connect with the feelings and needs of others.

- They have many problematic relationships with partners, family, friends, colleagues and neighbours.

- They present as selfish

- They take advantage of people. They tend to be serial cheats and liars.

- They resent other people's success and they believe

other people resent theirs.

- They demand that other people put their needs above everyone else.

- They are angry and upset if other people ignore them and don't give them what they feel they deserve.

This type of personality disorder can cause difficulties in many areas of life. It can lead to the narcissist becoming disillusioned and unhappy when their fantasies of fame and fortune do not materialise and they are not admired at the level to which they feel entitled. These feelings can turn them into chronic pessimists believing that the world is a bad place, full of inferior, jealous people who are out to get them.

What proportion of the population suffer from Narcissistic Personality Disorder? How long is a piece of string? There are various estimations but the most common seems to be something in the region of 1 in 10 suffering one of the Cluster B type personality disorders and approximately 1 in 100 of the population identified with Narcissistic Personality Disorder. However, that may well be a gross underestimation given that narcissists, don't usually self identify. They never think that they have a problem. They truly believe they are better than the rest of humankind because they ARE superior beings.

If a narcissist does arrive at therapy they are often able to manipulate psychiatrists into believing it's their victim who has the real problem. There seems to be a common consensus that therapy makes a narcissist worse, not better and the older they get the worse they become. It seems many are able to hone their manipulative skill as they age and therapy only helps them to become more skilled as they analyse the therapy itself and learn a new skill - how to manipulate a therapist! So unless their behaviour becomes extreme to the point of criminal, a narcissist can easily slip under the radar and never be identified let alone diagnosed.

There is an ongoing debate about whether narcissists are born with their tendencies or develop their problematic behaviour because of traumatic events or abuse during their childhood. The nature/nurture debate although fascinating is beyond the scope of this book, but whether a narcissist is born or made we can certainly agree that a narcissist has a way of thinking and reasoning that is different to the majority of the population.

Labelling people with narcissistic personality disorder however, is not particularly helpful. This book is not an attempt to armchair diagnose the problematic people in our lives. Although it is useful to name the types of Cluster B personality disorders and narcissistic traits in order to identify certain types of common behaviour it is probably not appropriate or of any real benefit to us, the victims, to label our difficult relationships. Whatever the clinical diagnosis may or may not be it's more important for us to recognise that this person has behaviours that are problematic for us and others. If we're living with a manipulative, pathological liar who is controlling aspects of our lives and making us unhappy, then we need to identify and address the issues. What is important is to realise that we are not imagining it or going crazy and that we can get help by educating ourselves. By learning the language of these damaging behaviours we are able to break free from the abuse, communicate effectively, gather support and emerge from the other side stronger and more enlightened.

Different types of narcissist

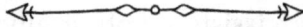

These narcissist types are not clinical definitions but they do help us to identify typical behaviour patterns.

- Overt or grandiose narcissists are usually extrovert and boastful for example, the type of behaviour demonstrated by Kanye West or Donald Trump may be defined as typical of overt narcissists. The type of narcissist portrayed in the media is usually in the Trump mould because he displays many of the traits that we would associate with the traditional type of narcissism. Showy, extrovert personality, not afraid to blow his own trumpet, the overt narcissist is easy to identify. They may be swaggering, boastful, full of stories about them-selves and prone to tantrums when they don't get their own way. In this respect they are the easiest to deal with because they are proud of their nar-cissistic tendencies, they don't feel the need to hide them and thus are easier to avoid. For the pur-poses of this book I intend to disregard the overt narcissist and focus on the hidden and cloaked varieties.

- The covert narcissist, also called the shy or vulner-able narcissist, can be charming, introverted and likeable.

- Cerebral narcissists are driven by academic

success, they feel their superiority stems from their intellect.

- Somatic narcissists are physically oriented. Body conscious, they are the type of narcissist who is most aligned with the Greek god of the original story, Narcissus.

- Delusional narcissists are full of wild stories that are so extreme few people would give them credibility. For example, they work in secret for the government but their cover is a day job at a burger joint.

- Malignant narcissists have traits of anti-social personality disorder and are arguably the most dangerous.

- Altruistic narcissists are pillars of the community. They go out of their way, or so it seems, to perform charitable works and good deeds. They 'love' animals and children.

Overt and covert narcissists may not know the term narcissist or ascribe it to themselves but they are definitely aware that they are different, in a superior way, to the rest of humanity. They may also recognise the emptiness within and their inability to connect to other people on any real emotional level. Real human relationships may be seen as a weakness or it may cause them genuine unhappiness when they realise that this aspect of life is missing for them. In either situation they will learn to use their lack of attachment to better manipulate and control the people around them.

The difference between overt and covert narcissism

is that, as the name suggests, the overt is open and has no problem with displaying their unlikable personality traits. Their grandiose behaviour is over the top and they don't care what people think of them. They will bulldoze everyone with their opinions, bully and abuse people and to hell with the consequences. This may make them unpleasant people to have contact with but at least we know what we're dealing with in all of their predictable unpredictability!

A covert narcissist, on the other hand, is unable to connect with people but they don't want anyone to discover this about them. They have become experts at concealing this aspect of their personality. They hide their real ambitions behind a veneer of acceptable and likeable behaviour, all the while amused at how easy it is to fool stupid people and get almost anything they want.

As small children, they will have learnt that they get a far better reaction if they are humble rather than brag. They go out of their way to perfect techniques that will improve their chances of getting the praise they need in order to bolster their self esteem. They find it difficult to regulate their own self esteem so they need validation to come from an outside sources. We all like praise, of course, but a narcissist needs it.

The coverts are also careful observers and may learn to mimic emotional displays in others in order to perform 'correctly' in any given situation. However, we occasionally sense the fakery; the crying without tears, the awkward hug, the smile that doesn't reach the eyes. Small things that our senses latch onto momentarily and feel 'off' before we dismiss them. We are recognising learned behaviours that have no real emotion to back them up.

When a narcissist is in a romantic relationship they will usually be exposed, eventually. They become bored and go on to their next source of supply leaving their victim hurt and confused. In this situation we may not have a name for the abuse but we definitely know we've been abused. We may not actually call them a narcissist but just use expletives!

If and when a narcissist finally puts down roots and creates a family it can be a different scenario. As a mature adult they may have decided that their best course of action will be to settle for what they have. This may be after several affairs or other escapades.

The narcissist will have 'trained' their partner to pander to their whims and they will now go out of their way to make this marriage or partnership work. On their own terms, of course. They will do everything to maintain their position, both in their family and in their community, whether that is their local council, community association and/or their social media presence. Their main preoccupation is for their narcissism to stay hidden and to maintain a public image. When they live within our own families they may be so expert at hiding their traits that it may be years, even decades before we realise their true nature.

The covert narcissist can present as a lovely person and may well bowl people over at first meeting with their understated charm. They may be humorous and disarmingly self deprecating. They are often skilled at job interviews - they are used to answering difficult questions with ease. They are the person who can justify anything and lying comes naturally to them, so in an interview situation they can usually blag their way into any job. They will effortlessly exaggerate their experience and qualifications. They may boast to their family and friends that they have been offered every job they have ever been interviewed for. The employer may be charmed initially by the narcissist but a few weeks down the line it may be a very different story when they are wondering how did I ever hire this unsuitable and inexperienced person?

Another facet of narcissism is the altruistic narcissist. It is said that true altruism does not exist. People who perform charitable or kind acts usually do them because it makes them feel good or special to a variable extent. Like narcissism itself this is a continuum, with most people on the low to medium scale and the altruistic narcissist at the upper end. A relationship with an altruistic narcissist can be especially confusing because the persona they project is one of generosity with an affinity for charitable work. It is difficult to attribute narcissistic qualities to someone who appears to be kind, giving and working selflessly for other people.

A clue that you may be dealing with an altruistic narcissist is that you will know a lot about their charitable work. You will know because they tell you and everyone else how good they are, how they work for nothing and that they just want to help everyone. They really put themselves out to help animals, children, the elderly and veterans. They ask for nothing in return and flaunt their generosity at every opportunity. They will attach themselves to high profile, social media friendly, charitable causes and will publish their involvement shamelessly. The broadcasting of this information gives them narcissistic supply as their group of acquaintances lavish them with high praise. This in turn reinforces their confidence in the belief that they are superior to others.

If they are financially secure they may even offer to work for no remuneration in a position that is usually paid.

The double bonus for doing for free what others charge for is that they receive even more kudos and supply from the organisation who employs them. But the biggest and most important advantage for the narcissist is that free work is an insurance against criticism. Who can criticise someone when they are giving their time and services freely? As we know the narcissist's ego is fragile and criticism is never welcomed, even if asked for, so trading a wage or fee for a position where their work cannot be evaluated or criticised will seem like a fair trade for some narcissists. In addition they may begin to criticise the people who do get paid to do what they do for free. It will be of no consequence to the narcissist that these people may have to put food on the table and that the provision of free work may undermine the opportunities of this particular group of workers. As long as they are able to criticise others and boost their own ego then all is good in the narcissist's world.

Caring and generous people do not announce their generosity, they don't have to sell themselves on social media as the most selfless people they know, and say with a virtual shrug, 'It's just the way I am' and 'Somebody has to do it'. It is also interesting to note that the people who shout the loudest about their 'good works' may also be receiving other benefits, either financially or in kind. If you look a little closer you may see that they are quietly promoting a product or service in the background for their own financial gain or are dipping into a charity's donations.

The narcissist within our own family circle, a parent, sibling, aunt or uncle, may have hidden in plain sight for many years. Sometimes they only become visible to us when we are researching narcissists because we suspect a friend or potential boyfriend/girlfriend is displaying problematic behaviour. It may be the case that a particular crisis has led to troubling behaviour and rather than just accepting it as we have in the past, we now are able to research and discover why our family member is acting in such an 'abnormal' manner.

As we dig deeper into researching we may recognise familiar behaviour patterns and suddenly realise we have been dealing with this for years. It can be a powerful and disturbing revelation as the scales fall from our eyes and we realise what has been going on under our noses. Everything begins to make sense and we realise that we have spent decades walking on eggshells to avoid confrontation with this person. We may have put aside our doubts and feelings of disquiet and made excuses for the narcissist. We may experience feelings of how could we have been so stupid not to ever realise this when it seems so obvious now?

As I've come to terms with this myself over several years I've realised that the narcissists that we're dealing with are experts at manipulation. They have been doing this all their lives, honing their skills in order to receive the attention that they so desperately need. We have been manipulated by experts into never questioning unusual behaviour, the lies, the not following through with commitments, the justification of any questionable conduct and the occasional outlandish, crazy, stories. They are proficient at these tactics and just because we fell for their lies doesn't make us stupid, just unfortunate.

LEARNING THE LANGUAGE

◁┼──────◇─o─◇──────┼▷

When we begin to look in any depth at narcissistic abuse we are presented with a new language to describe what can be unsettling and disturbing behaviours.

This terminology can be the key to recognition, acceptance and a stepping stone to moving on. Actions that were hard to grasp and too vague to explain, when grouped together become a behaviour that has a name.

We realise that we're not unique and that others have suffered in a similar way. We're not imagining things or losing our minds. These are some typical behaviour traits and techniques employed by narcissists and the associated terminology used to describe the narcissist's world.

Flying Monkeys/Enablers

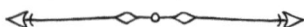

I prefer to use the term enablers, even though flying monkeys is the more popular description of this group of people who rush to the narcissist's defence and encourage their abusive behaviour.

Flying monkeys inject fantasy and a note of whimsy into a subject that is anything but cute and fantastical. The term originated from the film, starring Judy Garland, The Wizard of Oz. In the story the Wicked Witch controls a legion of flying monkeys who help her out by carrying out her evil deeds. With this army of helpers the Wicked Witch can wreak havoc on the people she hates without needing to get her hands dirty. It is an interesting side note that occasionally if an abuser is accused of narcissism they may appropriate the iconography in an attempt to control the situation. They may depict themselves as a flying monkey or witch to minimise, neutralise and mock the accusation.

In a narcissist's life enablers are important and they will often surround themselves with people who they consider to be vulnerable and gullible, who will fulfil this role. These are people who will take the narcissist at face value and are not going to delve into their background or ask difficult questions. This team of enablers may also include members of the narcissist's own close family, at least those who still remain. (Family members who have seen the mask slip and managed to break free from the manipulation may no longer have any contact with the narcissist.)

In my experience there are different types of enablers; the

first type are benign and are completely unaware of the narcissist's background and previous relationships. Often they are casual or new friends or possibly social media contacts. Narcissists have many new friends and contacts and usually these are short lived but intense relationships. Inevitably the new friend will infuriate or disappoint them and will be added to a long list of broken relationships.

There is also a practical component in the narcissist's inability to sustain long term friendships. They may move house many times in order to make fresh starts and these location changes are often dramatic. It's often not a move to trade up their home or a move to the next neighbourhood but rather hundreds or thousands of miles away and in a completely different type of environment. It may be an impromptu decision with no discernible reason to an outsider, they just need to get away to live in the city, or the country or by the sea. They will have every kind of justification for wanting to leave the area and considerations for their partner's job or child's education will have little bearing on their decision. Often they will have fantasies that in the new place they will be able to start again and their whole life will be different if they only lived in the city/owned a farm/ had a cottage next to a beach.

What is often going on behind the scenes is that the narcissist has been exposed or called out, maybe by a neighbour or colleague and it is imperative that they move away. They can't risk being exposed and humiliated in their own community. They need a fresh start in a new area.

Once established they will seek out people to continue the flow of narcissistic supply and this is where the new friend/benign enabler is useful. As human beings we seem set, by default, to believe what people tell us unless some other sense kicks in to warn us that this person might not be truthful. So a new contact will usually take anything that the narcissist tells them at face value. This may involve how they have been really unlucky in life because many of their previous relationships have been with crazy people, including members of their own family.

This is the reason, they explain, why they have little contact with significant family members, former friends, even their own children. They will prime this group of enablers with their back story and the new friends will usually support them in a dispute, in all innocence.

The second group of enablers are triggered by fear. They may not recognise it as such and might even laugh at the very notion. This group of enablers are often close family members or long-term friends. They are people who have plenty to lose if the 'love' or 'friendship' disintegrates. They are heavily invested in the relationship and need to keep it alive. If that means trash talking another family member or friend they will do it, rather than face the wrath of the narcissist. I use the word wrath carefully because as the closest family/friends they will have seen the narcissist at their worst. The temper tantrums when they don't get their own way, the punishments that may include the silent treatment, or the withdrawal of affection. This 'education' keeps the enabler in line. Tip-toeing and placating become second nature.

Adult family members then, may enable a narcissist for fear of being cut out of the family. This may seem extreme and unrealistic but the narcissist has no understanding, in real terms of 'unconditional love'. They are happy to use the term liberally on social networking sites in pretty pictorial quotations but, as the saying goes, they can talk the talk but can't walk the walk. The narcissist has no qualms in cutting a family member out of their lives completely and they are able to do this because they do not feel any genuine attachment. It's much easier for them to discard a relationship, even their own family member, when the victim is daring to disobey them. No more arguments, move on, never think of them again and they are able to accomplish this because of low levels of emotional maturity and their 'all or nothing' mentality.

Of course this won't be the public face they will show. They know what's acceptable to their public and for the narcissist it is vitally important to retain their public image. To a wider audience there will be justifications given *ad nauseam* to explain the situation. They will be heartbroken at how this has ended but they are the victim, of course. They just can't explain how it all came about and would give anything for it to be different.

So given this degree of manipulation, likely to have been played out many times in full view, it is not surprising that other close family members choose to enable the narcissist rather than risk being cut loose. In the beginning they may feel uncomfortable but as the years pass they fall into the role of narcissist protector without a second thought. They will be expected to defend the narcissist at all times and if they don't act quickly enough they will be called out,

"How can you let this person say that about your father?"

They are required to hold the same opinions, toe the line and come out fighting for the narcissist in any dispute.

It's not a given that every member of the narcissist's family will be an enabler. The more astute will have taken a step back. They don't want to become involved in the competitive and vindictiveness but neither do they want to initiate anger from the narcissist by severing the relationship. They may quietly drift away maintaining minimum contact in order not to risk a confrontation.

The narcissist may also organise regular family gatherings which serve to pull all members together as a group. This is a bonding exercise and also serves as a backdrop for the 'perfect family photos' that populate their social media sites. Conversations will centre on the common enemy, usually the latest family member to have been excluded. This will further cement the alliance between narcissist and their enablers and at the same time serves as a reminder and underlying threat that this could happen to any family member. You may be next.

A family gathering is also the perfect environment for the narcissist to quiz other family members and try to elicit any information about the now excluded member, that could be used against them. The narcissist might even throw out 'jokes' to test the strength of their enablers. "Imagine if someone slashed their tyres during the night!"

If one of the group takes the narcissist at their word and actually carries out the act in order to gain approval or advance their status in the group the narcissist may be faux outraged, "But I was only joking!" Secretly they will be delighted at this 'strike' on their enemy and the loyalty of their enabler.

This second type of enablers have been brainwashed and in many ways, even though they may be spiteful and vindictive we can see that fear is their motivation and feel a degree of sympathy for them.

Occasionally an incident may occur and it becomes obvious that the narcissist has no real feelings for the enabler at all. The friend or family member who has enabled the narcissist for many years may then break away and standing on the outside wonder how they could have been taken in for so long, and why isn't everyone else seeing it?

The third type of enablers are the malignant enablers. This group have bought into the narcissist's way of thinking wholesale. They are not being vindictive out of fear or innocence but because they have the same mindset as the narcissist. I'm not sure whether this is a meeting of two narcissists or if it is even possible for two narcissists to have a successful relationship? Can a narcissist mould another person into a narcissist? Possibly the second type of enabler, the fearful and dependent, gradually morph into the third type as a survival mechanism. If an enabler has decided to stay in the narcissist's world maybe it's a case of if you can't beat them join them. After many years it may be impossible to tell who was the original narcissist in this relationship.   I don't have a definitive answer and if you have known a partnership like this since the beginning of their relationship it's worth thinking back to when they first met. Did they both have narcissistic tendencies or did one influence the other?

Baiting

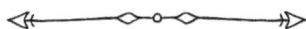

Narcissists can be adept at baiting their victim which serves an important function for maintaining their public image. If they can taunt their victim enough to get them to respond, particularly if they are also able to do this surreptitiously they can then publicise the victim's response and portray themselves as the eternal victim, i.e. look at this crazy person attacking me for no reason at all.

It's not uncommon for narcissists to bait people out of boredom. Their lack of empathy means that they have no qualms using others for the purpose of their own entertainment. Have you ever seen the TV show Catfish? This 'reality show' investigates people who create fake personal profiles online. Known as 'catfish' these online fakers often steal photographs and biographical information from other internet users to create an attractive profile. The "catfish" then uses this persona to trick unsuspecting people into a romantic relationship. When the 'fish' is finally caught and confronted their reaction is often one of 'so what?' Some even admit they created the profile out of boredom just to have some fun and they appear to have no awareness of the harm they have caused toying with another person's emotions. They show no remorse because they don't think they've done anything wrong. They were just having fun.

Incidentally part of the show involves a follow up with the perpetrator of the abuse the next day when they are usually full of regret for their behaviour. One suspects that they have either had time to fully comprehend how this show will impact their life or a producer has taken them to one side and explained. Now they display remorse.

The caveat here is that this a reality show that may or may not be scripted, but either way it is an interesting display of behaviour that is also common with narcissists.

As well as disturbing antics online, it is not uncommon for narcissists to amuse themselves by playing cruel pranks in order to humiliate an empathetic or vulnerable person in 'real life'. A narcissist will find it deliciously entertaining and if this is within a family setting the abuser will constantly remind the victim at every family gathering. Remember when you (insert humiliating incident here) and they will take great delight in reliving it over and over again, hoping for a negative response from the victim. Baiting - the gift that keeps on giving.

Cognitive Dissonance

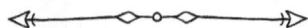

This is a state of mind that occurs when two conflicting beliefs are held at the same time, resulting in a feeling of discomfort or uneasiness.

In a relationship with a narcissist this can occur when you hold one belief about a person, for example this is my mother with all the associated feelings of the love of a parent and how society portrays a mother's behaviour but you also know that your mother is treating you badly. This is not how a mother should behave to her child. You may start to justify her bad behaviour to yourself and invent excuses. Otherwise this relationship makes no sense and, particularly as an adult, why would you tolerate it?

Looking back on my involvement with a narcissist I can see that I made excuse after excuse for their puzzling behaviour in an effort to make sense of a relationship that now, with the benefit of hindsight seems incredibly one-sided.

I admired them and brushed aside any doubts about the way they interacted with other people, not least with myself. However, I was often surprised when people I knew expressed reservations about my friend. Unlike me they hadn't received the years of 'training' nor had they needed to master the art of cognitive dissonance. I was blinded to the dubious behaviour and doubted the instincts of my more perceptive friends and family who had immediately picked up that there was something 'off' in this relationship.

Devalue and discard

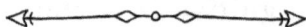

This is the end stage of a relationship when the narcissist will devalue their victim before discarding them completely.

In a family relationship this may only become apparent when the narcissist has been publicly exposed for their behaviour and a crisis occurs, but the devaluing may have been going on for years or even decades.

The narcissist is all too aware that one day they may be exposed for who they really are and that this could shatter the fragile persona that they have crafted so carefully. Damage limitation will have been taking place. If they can badmouth their target before the truth is told, anything their victim says about them will be diminished. When the discard occurs and the relationship ends the narcissist may immediately start a smear campaign in order to pre-empt what they believe is the upcoming war. They are terrified that their victim will start to reveal their secrets and they will be prepared to begin dishing any dirt they have collected on their target. Of course whatever snippets of information they can dig up will be exaggerated and turned to their advantage. They will be puzzled if their victim doesn't retaliate against their 'revelations' because they find it difficult to imagine that not everybody would behave in the same manipulative way that they do.

The discard itself can take several forms but the narcissist will often just disappear from a victim's life. In a non-romantic relationship it can be simply withdrawing themselves from the relationship on every level. They may not answer phone calls, texts or emails and may block and ban their victim on every social media platform, as if they never existed.

When a victim looks back to analyse exactly what happened it seems ridiculously trivial. They dared to disagree with the narcissist, or they continued in a relationship that the narcissist disapproved of. This will be the narcissistic injury that engendered the rage and the real reason the discard happened. How dare you disagree or disobey them? The narcissistic ego will not allow this kind of transgression in their own family.

However, even a narcissist will realise that for a wider audience this is a thin reason for destroying a relationship. It's at this stage they can fall back on the bank of devaluation, the 'insurance' they've been building up, possibly for years. The current transgression will be the 'straw that broke the camel's back', at least, in their retelling of the story. It will be last in a long line of misdemeanours committed against the narcissist over many years. They are the victim in this and are too stressed to deal with it anymore.

Narcissists will not allow themselves to be discarded. They always need to be seen to be the person ending the relationship, even going so far as to hoover the victim back into the fold if they sense they are about to leave. Then they will reject their victim, maybe just days later. Such is their ego that they need to convince themselves and others, that it was them that put an end to the relationship.

Dog Whistles

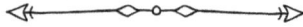

Dog whistle posting on social media platforms is a common tactic of the covert narcissist, in an attempt to procure a reaction from their victim.

The term is taken from a type of whistle used to train dogs, invented in 1876 by Francis Galton. The whistle emits sound in the ultrasonic range which people are unable to hear but some animals can, including dogs and cats. It can be used in their training without disturbing any humans present.

Currently the term is most commonly used to describe political statements that employ coded language, for example, an article that appears to mean something benign to the general population but provokes a negative response from a targeted sector of society. Most people who read it will think it's innocent, but there is an ulterior motive at play.

The narcissist may be particularly adept at using this technique in a social media setting to provoke a response or shame their victim.

For example, maybe the devalued and discarded family member had shoplifted as a child many years earlier. Nobody in their current life or family know anything about it. However, the narcissist is aware that, even though it would seem trivial to many people, their victim still feels a sense of shame and wouldn't want their spouse or children knowing about it. The covert narcissist, with their smear, taunting and goading campaign well under way may search Google for an article about childhood shoplifters. Ideally, it would conclude by saying that children who steal end up becoming monsters, or some other equally negative outcome. If you search hard enough you can come up with words to suit almost any viewpoint. The narcissist will post that article on their social media page with mock seriousness and concern, "How sad, isn't this terrible?" and in their own eyes they have won twice. Firstly here's another fake concern article that their group will love. It's not written by them but by an 'expert'. They are only posting something that may be of general interest to others, they tell themselves as they flutter their eyelashes. In addition they've managed to land a blow on their discard that is hidden to others. The narcissist will rejoice in causing pain to their victim by signalling, look I know what you did and I could reveal it at any time.

However, this does have an opportunity to backfire if the narcissist's group is large and the "crime" they're commenting on is either trivial or is a subject that they don't fully understand. For example one of their group might comment, "Hey I shoplifted as a child but I got caught, learnt my lesson and I never did it again. I'm an upstanding member of the community now so I think your article isn't fair or accurate." The narcissist will then have to backtrack, and say something like, "Oh I didn't mean YOU .." and try to find some way of saving face." Watching the narcissist struggle to regain control of the situation can be a rare moment of humour for the narcissist's victim as the abuser will twist and turn in an effort not to offend their group members.

Gaslighting

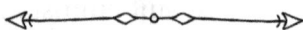

Gaslighting is a form of emotional abuse used to alter a person's perception of reality. It is a deliberately manipulative behaviour designed to sow the seeds of self doubt, persuading the victim to trust the abuser and to have misgivings about their own sanity.

The term comes from the play and film of the same name starring Ingrid Bergman and Charles Boyer. Boyer, the abusive husband begins to make his wife, Bergman believe she is insane by altering her environment and then telling her she is delusional when she notices the changes. This crazy-making manipulation is used by narcissists who will argue that black is white and that they didn't say something or do something that you clearly heard or saw them say or do. A similar technique to brainwashing, the perpetrator will use kindness to allay suspicions and act as if they are concerned for the victim's mental health. They may be faux sympathetic and tell their victim that that they are 'losing it' in an affectionate - don't worry, I'll look after you - kind of way. If the abuser is challenged they might become indignant or feign hurt.

This manipulation is an attempt to distort reality, they may even provide doctored evidence that their victim is wrong about what they remembered. It is a seriously disturbing mind game because ultimately the victim begins to question their own memory, senses and sanity. In addition they may feel guilty for doubting someone who apparently cares for them in many other ways.

A victim of this type of abuse may no longer trust their own judgement. They may lose confidence and find it increasingly difficult to challenge the narcissist as they come to doubt their own mental health. It may only be with hindsight, after the relationship has come to a crisis point or ended, that they are able to look back with some objectivity and see how they have been exposed to this insidious behaviour.

Ghosting

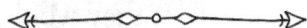

An alternative term for the discard but often more dramatic. Ghosting is when someone suddenly cuts off all contact with no explanation and they appear to have vanished from the face of the earth.

The Golden Child and the Scapegoat

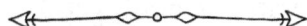

In a family dynamic, the idealisation can take place over many years and if this is a family with narcissist parents they may use the roles of 'golden child' and 'scapegoat'.

Creating the role of golden child can be a cynical ploy. The narcissist may be planning for their old age even when their family are small children. They may be looking to see which child they can groom to be the one that will look after them as they age. This will be the child who will never move far from home. Once they have been identified as the golden child he or she can do no wrong and conversely the scapegoat will be blamed for any and all problems that occur within the family unit. Having someone to blame for everything that goes wrong allows the rest of the family to buy into the illusion that they are emotionally and psychologically healthier than the scapegoat. They rarely have to take responsibility for any wrongdoings when there is a scapegoat around to absorb the bumps of family life.

Having a scapegoat child in the family also allows an environment where the narcissistic father or mother never have to question their role as the 'perfect parent'. In their minds the only fly in the ointment of their otherwise flawless family is the scapegoat. If they would only get their act together, everything could be wonderful.

Other children in the family follow their parent's cue. They quickly realise that they can get out of trouble and form tighter bonds with the rest of the family by targeting and bullying the scapegoat. From this foundation family lore is contrived with the scapegoat at the centre of a well established script. In adulthood the myths of the scapegoat's 'crimes' are rehashed and exaggerated at family get-togethers. If the family come together over Sunday lunch it is very likely that the black sheep and all their faults will be discussed, *ad nauseam*.

Emotionally healthy people might find this kind of discussion uncomfortable, particularly as it is likely to take place on a regular basis. Instead of being asked questions about their lives or their week at work they are again discussing the 'crimes' of their sibling. This will likely take place in a family setting with younger members present, who although they may not be active in the conversation, are able to absorb the information that, for example, their aunt or uncle must be a very bad person.

The discussion and shared hatred will give the narcissist a warm glow and as they are never contradicted by their family they will feel that, once again, they have the moral high ground and have been right in their actions to exclude the target of their wrath. They will revel in their tight knit, united family.

In addition to getting their fill of narcissistic supply this kind of cosy, 'bash the scapegoat' get together also serves as a warning. Whilst the bonding may engender temporary positive feelings there may also be an underlying impression of unease that if you don't 'toe the line' then this will also be your fate. Your life will be taken apart in forensic detail, siblings will be grilled for any information that they have about you and the resulting sharing of information will form the basis of a mock fest. "Oh did you hear they did this? What a loser . . . they were always a loser though, weren't they?"

The 'golden child' will be lauded, particularly on social media and will be kept closer than the others, even as an adult. This is the narcissist's insurance for old age. The favoured child may well be promised financial rewards as an inducement but often it's the psychological, reciprocal arrangement they have that is what binds. They have made the adult child dependent on them in many ways and even if they want to move away, either physically or psychologically, always at the back of their minds is the treatment meted out to the scapegoat.

With their own parents or other ageing relatives, the narcissist may strategically put physical distance between them in order to avoid any caring responsibilities. They will give chapter and verse as to how caring they are but as we see time and time again with narcissists, their actions do not match their words. They're not actually going to DO anything to help. Moving away is not an accident, but a strategy. Covert narcissists often plan many years ahead and then, "Oh dear, its so unfortunate that I can't do more to help. If only I wasn't so far away."

Conversely if their own children decide to move away they may follow them. They know this trick and they're not going to have it played on them. They will come up with all sorts of reasons and justifications to move near to the favoured child and as we have come to realise they are the masters of justification. However, at the root of this plan is the sheer panic they face at abandonment and the loss of their potential 'carer'. This type of forward planning will not usually be vocalised, even to their own partners. They realise the genuine reasons are needy and selfish. However, in their own heads they are able to justify it and end up believing their own lies, which is one of the reasons they are so good at convincing others.

The golden child has been groomed from an early age and is seen to be receiving all the love and attention engendering feelings of resentment in their siblings. However, all that favouritism has a price to pay. By the time they are middle-aged they are so entrenched in their parent's world they have no chance of an independent life. Ultimately the 'golden child' may pay the highest price to narcissistic parents. Conversely, in the end the scapegoat may become the luckiest child, rejected by the family they can be their own person, free of the malignant influence of the narcissist.

Hoovering

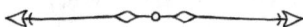

Hoovering is a term for a technique used by narcissists to get back into your life. This may happen after they have discarded you or when you have initiated no-contact and it can happen days, months or even years after the event.

They may contact you completely out of the blue and in some cases as if nothing has ever happened. If you bring up the past they will use phrases like, "lets leave the past in the past", "we can make a fresh start" and if they are a family member they may even use that old favourite, "blood is thicker than water".

They will demonstrate, in this initial contact, everything that you used to love about them. They are also likely to appeal to shared memories, 'Remember when we.. '. They will use every trick in the book to appeal to friend or family love and loyalty and may know you well enough to break down your defences.

What we need to remember in these circumstances is that they are highly skilled. This is how they live their lives every day, they have practised their manipulative skills many, many times. Even though we may feel older, wiser and stronger the narcissist is likely to be more adept and/or desperate than the last time you had contact.

Only you can make the decision to believe them when they say they've changed, or that the incident that caused you to separate was just a blip, an unimportant pot hole in the road of family or friendship.

If you dig a little deeper you may discover that something has gone wrong for them lately, maybe they've been thrown out of their relationship, home or job. They may need somewhere to live, or a source of money and they are looking for a replacement narcissistic supply to provide it. You!

As they get older the narcissist realises that their

appearance and charms are waning and they will now be looking for someone to care for them in their declining years. They may use ageing, frailty and ill health to make you feel guilty enough to resume your relationship. However, if you have any doubts at all I would urge you to seek out the narcissist abuse survivors forums and share your concerns with others before you let a narcissist back into your life.

It's worth noting that, just to confuse matters, a narcissist may also employ fake hoovering techniques. This can be observed on social networking sites in a public but invariably false attempt at reconciliation. They will not approach their victim privately but instead make a public post briefly explaining to their 'fans' about the trauma caused by their victim . They will be suitably vague, talking about the stress, the sleepless nights, etc but even after all they have suffered, all they wish for is reconciliation. Because, you know, life is short. In a public post they can demonstrate to their followers, once again that they are the victim in this scenario, but they are still prepared to try and put this right and offer reconciliation. They are the better person. However, in reality the motivation for this act is purely to shore up their public image. They lay traps baited with possibilities of resolution without any real intention of following through and they pepper the bait with negativity, veiled insults and conditions. The negativity will go largely unnoticed by their group and once again they will have turned the knife a little deeper, safe in the knowledge that the dog whistles included in their post will have guaranteed that their victim will almost certainly not respond. This is the perfect outcome for the narcissist. In reality they don't want to move towards reconciliation, at least not unless their victim is willing to adhere to their conditions. The tactic of appearing to be the bigger person and at the same time undermining any genuine attempt to restore harmony et voila, the narcissist is able to emerge both the hero and the victim.

Mobbing

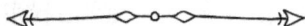

One of the most disturbing displays to witness on social networking sites is that of mobbing.

Mobbing is a term used to describe a form of bullying by a group of people who gather together to attack and emotionally abuse their victim by their use of intimidation and humiliation or discrediting and isolating them. The group leader, in this case, will be the narcissist who coerces his group of enablers into mobbing their selected victim. The leader will look for individuals who are not narcissists themselves, but rather emotionally immature individuals often with poor moral values; the wannabes. They will be motivated to take on the dirty work of the narcissist and as detailed later, we can see how that plays out, before our eyes, both in day to day life and in writing on various social media platforms. Bully Online* describes the difference between bullying and mobbing :

The word bullying is used to describe a repeated pattern of negative intrusive violational behaviour against one or more targets and comprises constant trivial nit-picking criticism, refusal to value and acknowledge, undermining, discrediting and a host of other behaviours …

"Mobbing" involves a group of people whose size is constrained by the social setting in which it is formed…. It might

* What Is Mobbing and What's the Difference between Mobbing and Bullying? http://bullyonline.org/old/workbully/mobbing.htm. Accessed 27 July 2018.

seem to the target as if many people are involved but in reality the group might be small. The group members directly interact with a target in an adversarial way that undermines or harms them in measurable, definable ways.

The word mobbing is preferred to bullying in continental Europe and in those situations where a target is selected and bullied (mobbed) by a group of people rather than by one individual. However, every group has a ringleader. If this ringleader is an extrovert it will be obvious who is coercing group members into mobbing the selected target. If the ringleader is an introvert type, he or she is likely to be in the background coercing and manipulating group members into mobbing the selected target; introvert ringleaders are much more dangerous than extrovert ringleaders.

In a mobbing situation, the ringleader incites supporters, cohorts, copycats and unenlightened, inexperienced, immature or emotionally needy individuals with poor values to engage in adversarial interaction with the selected target. The ringleader, or chief bully, gains gratification from encouraging others to engage in adversarial interaction with the target. "

A common tactic used by mobs is body shaming public posts, for example, calling their victim ugly, fat or any other feature they deem to be worthy of highlighting and mocking. They are often creative with their insults and will use visual aides, such as cartoons and gifs, to get their point across. As each member of the group comments, the insults become more hurtful and obscene as they appear to compete with each other to be the most offensive. We might imagine that this kind of abuse is only prevalent amongst young teenagers using social media. We may generalise that teenagers are emotionally immature and may not realise the consequences that this sort of sustained attack can have on a person's emotional well being. However, the narcissist is low on the emotional intelligence scale and seriously wants to damage their target and in this case we may see elderly parents and their adult children team up in an attempt to destroy a family member.

Surprisingly, there appears to be no correlation between the 'beauty' of the attacker and the 'ugliness' of the victim. The narcissist is blind to their own lack of socially acceptable conventional attractiveness, but conversely will be extremely sensitive to any criticism directed at the way they look.

The narcissist who is guarding their public image carefully may pull back if it looks to others that they are involved in bullying. They may gather their mob to harass their victims in a relatively subtle manner by publishing a general post in a way that is harder to address. For example a narcissist will post a picture of an ugly animal and laugh about the poor creature with their friends. However, the narcissist, their enablers and the victim knows what is really being said. The animal is likely to have an exaggerated feature that the victim is sensitive about and the comments from the mob will all be centred on that feature.

If questioned about their behaviour the narcissist will deny any knowledge that this is about the victim. They are likely to feign innocence .Who me? They are just having a joke with their friends. In this way they can bully the victim, eating away at their self esteem without ever being challenged. They may even boast about their clever bullying tactic to others. "Nobody can prove anything, I never call them by their name so it's fine. I could be talking about anyone."

Narcissistic Injury

According to the Diagnostic and Statistical Manual of Mental Disorders (DSM -5) narcissistic injury can be described as [†]

"Vulnerability in self-esteem which makes narcissistic people very sensitive to 'injury' from criticism or defeat. Although they may not show it outwardly, criticism may haunt these individuals and may leave them feeling humiliated, degraded, hollow and empty. They react with disdain, rage, or defiant counterattack."

Narcissists are extremely sensitive not just to any kind of criticism, real or perceived but even minor disagreement or differences of opinion. Generally they feel they know everything about anything that they're interested in and they cannot be taught anything new, especially by people who are inferior to them, ie everyone. They will feel outraged if someone suggests otherwise and points out deficiencies in their knowledge and the injury will be palpable. Similarly, a narcissist can be injured if he receives even the slightest criticism in public, including on social networking sites.

Narcissistic Rage

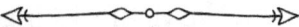

Narcissistic rage occurs when a narcissist has been thwarted in their plans for world domination, or domination of you and they lose control.

[†] Diagnostic And Statistical Manual of Mental Disorders : DSM-5. Arlington, VA :American Psychiatric Publishing, 2013.

You may have disobeyed them, lined the cups up incorrectly in the cupboard, or pointed out a home truth about their narcissistic tendencies. Narcissistic rage exposes the highly inflated levels of entitlement and false sense of superiority. It's at this stage that they let their real feelings and attitudes surface and their dysfunction is exposed.

Christine Louis de Canonville writes on her blog Narcissistic Behaviour[‡]

"The rages can take two forms: explosive and pernicious, or passive-aggressive. The explosive and pernicious rages are highly volatile outbursts which may be verbal or physical, whereas the passive-aggressive rages are more likely to be experienced when the narcissist withdraws into sulky silent treatment as a means of punishment."

Narcissistic rage is not the same as anger which is normally directed towards a specific issue or source. The hyper-vigilant narcissist suffers with paranoia, thinking that people are continually plotting and planning against them. They believe that everyone has a similar mindset to their own and as they spend a large proportion of their lives conspiring against others, then it follows that others are behaving in a similar fashion. Consequently they are always on guard, looking for imagined slights, disguised insults and conspiracies. It doesn't take much to provoke an explosion when their lives are lived on a hair-trigger. They have a low tolerance for frustration and if they are thwarted, contradicted or publicly humiliated they will react in a similar fashion to a 4 year old child being denied a promised treat. This behaviour in an adult is dramatic and they can flip in an instant from Mr Nice

---

‡ Christine Louis de Canonville.What Is Narcissistic Rage?https:// narcissisticbehavior.net/what-causes-narcissistic-rage/. Accessed 27 July 2018.

Guy to all out, 100 mile an hour tantrum which may involve screaming and shouting, throwing and breaking objects, threats of violence and actual violence. Of course they never take responsibility for their actions, and 'you made me do it' is their typical reaction during the aftermath.

Some of the narcissist's behaviour is at an infantile level because they have not been able to mature, emotionally. Although narcissists will mock and devalue sensitivity in others they are highly sensitive to criticism themselves. If you disagree with them or fight back when they attack, you they may well lose control and this can be a dangerous time if you are confronting a narcissist with violent tendencies. The rage that a covert narcissist experiences may also be turned inwards if they are in a situation where their public image may be compromised by a display of anger. They may channel their incandescent rage into passive aggressive behaviours, plot detailed revenge scenarios or present displays of victimisation or self pity. They will be relentless in their pursuit of winning; they feel that their life depends on this battle and they will fight to the end even if it means destroying themselves in the process.

To further confuse the issue there are also narcissists who use cold rage to manipulate those around them. If they are in a situation and feel they are losing control they may appear to lose their temper, shout and scream in rage in a dramatic manner but will be able to stop immediately and walk away with a smirk. If they are losing an argument they know that exploding in temper can intimidate and put an end to any debate so they may use a fake tantrum whenever it suits the situation.

Narcissistic Supply

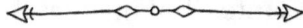

This is a concept used to describe the type of admiration and support required by a narcissist to maintain their self esteem. Unlike most people, it is impossible for a narcissist to regulate their own self worth so they need it to be bolstered by outside sources. This can be family members who continually need to reassure the narcissist that they are clever/talented/beautiful - depending on the type of narcissism, ie cerebral, somatic etc.

"Mirror, mirror on the wall, who is the fairest of them all?" In a family situation the other members are the narcissist's mirror used to reflect and enhance the narcissist's self esteem whenever required. Any attention feeds the narcissist's needs, both positive or negative so the drama and chaos that they cultivate also serves to augment their supply.

Often narcissists crave attention from strangers to bolster their supply and in many ways this is easy to obtain, particularly through the medium of social networking sites. Appearances matter much more than truth or substance, so the narcissist will manufacture or exaggerate their achievements. They may rewrite history distorting the facts to make themselves appear more interesting. They will become either a hero and gain supply from adoration, or a victim and soak up the pity and support given by people who don't know them but have natural empathy. They will exaggerate their talents and skills in whatever way they can get away with to gain attention. As a would-be writer or artist they may steal other's work and pass it off as their own because most of their followers will not realise the truth. As long as they can get praise from the majority with only a few suspecting they can even fool themselves into thinking that they are unique and special.

No Contact

‹‹————◇–∘–◇————››

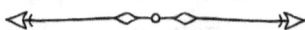

No contact is a term used to break all bonds between the victim and their narcissistic friend or family member. It is arguably the only effective and permanent way to put an end to narcissistic nonsense and abuse. This can be difficult to maintain because of the strong attachment felt by the victim of narcissistic abuse, particularly if the abuser uses hoovering techniques in an attempt to rekindle the relationship. However, if this can be accomplished it can give the victim time and space to heal and rebuild their life.

Grey Rock

‹‹————◇–∘–◇————››

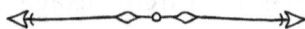

Grey rock is a term first used by Skylar[§] on the website 180 Rule.

Going 'grey rock' is a technique that has proved

---

§ Skylar. 'The Gray Rock Method of Dealing With Psychopaths'. 180 RULE, 30 Mar. 2012, https://180rule.com/the-gray-rock-method-of-dealing-with-psychopaths/.

useful for dealing with a narcissist when it's impossible to go fully 'no-contact'. It's a way to handle communication with a narcissist if, for example, the victim has to co-parent with the abuser and needs to have contact with them regarding their child.

The advice is to keep everything as low key as possible, don't say anything that might provoke, don't respond to provocation and just become as boring as possible. Speak in a flat tone and keep your answers to questions as monosyllabic as possible. The theory is that the narcissist craves excitement, and if you're not providing any excitement they will become bored and look elsewhere for their supply.

Object Constancy

Object constancy is a term used to describe the ability that we can know something exists even if we can't see it. For example, a young child will learn that their parent will return after a period of separation and as they get older, the time periods apart can gradually increase without creating trauma in the child.

Psychological object constancy is the ability to preserve a favourable emotional attachment to someone, even if you are annoyed or angry with their behaviour.

So we can have an argument with our partner and feel

really angry, but at the same time we know that this one dis-agreement is not going to be the end because of the deep attachment and love underpinning the relationship. The narcissist generally has a poor level of object constancy and is unable to hold those two conflicting opinions about them-selves or other people at the same time. This manifests itself when they identify another person as special and perfect but are then dismayed or even disgusted to find a flaw in the "saint's" character or behaviour. One disagreement or argument can signal the complete end of a relationship with a narcissist because they are unable to see the positives in the relationship.

Love bombing/idealisation

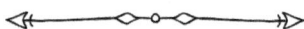

Although in a family or friend relationship we do not encounter the typical love bombing that occurs in a romantic relationship, such as rushing intimacy, we may experience a period of idealisation. This type of 'all or nothing' behaviour can stem from the narcissist who has extreme views that they will not deviate from, no matter how persuasive the argument. There are no grey areas for them and this is demonstrated in terms of relationships with a love or hate mentality.

An example is when a narcissistic meets someone who is a potential new friend, they will enthuse about them to the point of extreme. They will tell their family and other friends incessantly what a wonderful person this person is and list everything about them that is positive. Their jokes are the funniest, they have the best taste in clothes, the best job, etc.

They are likely to let other people down in order to spend more time with their new best friend.

However, inevitably this idealisation period won't last. Something will be said or done that to the average person will be a trivial remark or disagreement, but to the narcissist will be a fatal wound and because they suffer from a lack of object constancy they will discard that relationship. It doesn't matter if the person was a 'close' family member or a relative stranger the discard will be same. The caveat here is that if the narcissist needs something from this person, money or status, for example, they may rekindle the relationship at some point in the future and at the same time criticise the victim behind their back for their failings and mock them for their gullibility. There is an inability to deviate from perfection on the narcissist's part and they expect their friend and family relationships to match their own perfect but fabricated image of themselves. Naturally, this leads to many fragmented relationships and you may observe that a middle aged narcissist has no friends from their past and only transient friendships in the present.

Orbiting

Orbiting is a behaviour that happens frequently, not just with narcissists but it is a favourite trick after they have discarded or ghosted their victim. Anna Iovine, from the website Dating Trend⁵, who coined the term describes it as someone

⁵ Iovine, Anna. 'Dating Trend: Orbiting Someone Is the New Ghosting Someone'. Man Repeller, 23 Apr. 2018, https://www.manrepeller.com/2018/04/orbiting-is-the-new-ghosting.html.

'keeping you in their orbit — close enough to see each other; far enough to never talk.'

Online, on social networking sites, the narcissist might block and/or ban their victim immediately after the discard but then use a fake account to watch them. They will stalk the target's feeds regularly in order to gather information. They may then save the details to use in the future. This may involve dog whistle posts specifically referring to their victim's feed in order to intimidate them. They will always be watching.

Passive Aggression

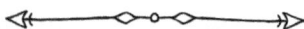

B eing passive aggressive comes naturally to the narcissist. They hate confrontation, and as a child it's likely that they were made to suppress any angry emotions. If they themselves were raised by narcissistic parents confrontation about anything would have been taboo and often punished.

As an adult then, they will avoid confrontation at all costs. In order to deal with anger without confrontation they will find other, more sneaky ways and these can take a number of different forms. They may sabotage the person they are angry with in all manner of ways, for example, using subtle actions like deliberately making them late for an important appointment.

This kind of behaviour can make living with a narcissist confusing. If they are angry at you, lots of little things may start going wrong in your life but you will have no idea what's happening. It's only with hindsight that you may recognise a pattern. The narcissist will make sure they leave no trace and will never be able to be pulled up on these sabotage actions. It satisfies their anger somewhat to be constantly tripping up the person they want to make miserable and they will be laughing to themselves at how stupid their victim is not to realise what they're doing.

Other passive aggressive behaviour might manifest itself when the narcissist pretends to be interested in, for example, volunteering for a charity. When the time comes they don't want to be upfront, say no and damage their reputation as a charitable person, instead they will always have a good excuse not to follow through.

There are many other ways that a narcissist may show passive aggression, for example, playing loud music if they know that you're studying and then fake concern that they didn't realise you could hear it or that it would bother you.

They may also play music with messages. They study the lyrics of songs to find the perfect words to suit any occasion. Unable to articulate what they feel and finding direct confrontation impossible, they will play the perfect lyrics over and over hoping you will get the message but denying that's what they're doing if questioned. "I just like this song", shrug. They will secretly be smirking that you have identified the message and they have been able to get that across to you without saying anything at all.

The silent treatment is another passive aggressive tactic. Withdrawing themselves is the ultimate non-confrontation but also guarantees confusion and upset in the victim. They may just ignore the victim at home, pretending that they haven't spoken and sulking like a small child. If we consider that their emotional maturity is at the same level as a toddler, this makes sense but it is still difficult to deal with. If you don't live with the narcissist, they may storm out of your house if they're unhappy with you and this could be during the most minor disagreement or anything that they may, with their heightened sensitivity and paranoia, consider a slur.

A cerebral narcissist might storm out if they have lost playing a board game. A semantic narcissist might leave in a huff if he is outperformed at the gym by someone he considers inferior. Slamming doors and other forms of aggression to objects rather than people is another type of passive aggression.

Leaving in a temper and then withdrawing from contact is another powerful form of passive aggression, leaving the victim hurt and confused with a 'what the hell just happened here?' feeling. An emotionally healthy person, the first time this happens, might treat it as an aberration and be expecting contact later that day with an apology. Not so for a narcissist. For them the incident has ruined the relationship completely. You have caused them to expose themselves and the relationship is no longer the perfect and idealised relationship it once was. For the narcissist that is the end, forever. There can be no going back and they will shrug you off and move on to pastures new. They were never attached to you, just the idea of you and the perfect friendship, but they were never there emotionally. They move on without a backward glance.

The caveat here is if you are providing them with narcissistic supply that they can't find immediately elsewhere, for example money or a roof over their head. In these circumstances they may manipulate you into asking them to return so they can rekindle the relationship in the short term. However, this will be the beginning of the end for them and they will be lining up new sources of supply as they begin to devalue you in preparation for the inevitable discard.

Projection

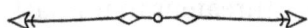

Projection, in psychological terms, is the process where people defend against their own negative qualities by denying them in themselves and attributing these qualities to others. For example if someone feels that they have a tendency to be intolerant, they might never address this openly about themselves, but instead will criticise those around them for being intolerant.

Over the years, in order to compensate for the emptiness and lack of any real feeling, they have built a 'perfect' version of themselves in their mind. This person may be the 'salt of the earth', charitable, kind to animals and kids and loved by all. On some level they know that this is really not who they are, but they suppress those feelings and do whatever they can to avoid them surfacing. One method that helps to alleviate these terrifying feelings is to project any of the 'failing' parts of themselves onto others. For example, they may be all about accumulating money, but they hide their real ambitions behind a facade that includes embracing the simple life and working for charity. They may then project their real feelings onto others by accusing them of being greedy, money-grabbing and encouraging their enablers to judge people's worth according to their level of charity work. In this particular competition the narcissist is the winner, of course.

At a deeper level the narcissist is terrified of being abandoned and feels that they are worthless. They know that these are deeply unattractive traits however and they fight to hide them every day of their lives. They put on their false self and steel themselves to face the world, determined that nobody will ever glimpse the real person beneath the attractive shell.

When someone threatens to unmask a narcissist we can see how this might give them the motivation to fight hard to disprove this slur on their character. Their public image is at stake. Rather than dismiss or ignore it, this kind of accusation is likely to trigger the cerebral narcissist to begin a research project to deflect the claim and project it back onto their accuser. One concerning aspect of projection is if they are accusing you of being a narcissist. It is likely they will put in an incredible amount of work to prove to their 'public' (their most important audience) that they are the true victims. They will study websites, contribute to forums, even make their own videos about the topic and will soak up all the experiences of real victims to use themselves in their own twisted and manipulative presentation. Now they have a name for their 'abuser's' disorder, the motivation and most likely a loyal group of enablers to back them up.

The narcissist's acts of projection can have long lasting consequences. In one example a man had convinced his therapist that he was the victim of a narcissist, his wife. The therapist treated the man's wife with a degree of hostility and was working with them both to resolve the situation. It only emerged many years later that the true narcissist was the husband and his wife had not only endured a lifetime of humiliation and narcissistic rage from her husband but had been re-traumatised by the therapist.

The Selective Listener

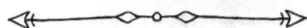

Narcissists can be attentive listeners but only for their own purposes. In the early stages of a relationship they will be engrossed in conversations and hang on every word of a potential new friend or colleague. However, they're not doing this because they are interested in the other person in any conventional sense but rather they need to gather as much information as possible in order to become what that person needs or doesn't need in a relationship. They will mirror interests, desires and ambitions. The challenge for the narcissist is to become the perfect potential friend or colleague in order to gain trust and ultimately narcissistic supply. They also need to extract as much information as possible about their victim's life and background, past relationships and problems. They will be banking this information, particularly any weaknesses, which they can and will use against their victims at a later stage.

Once they have hooked their prey they will relax into the relationship and often become completely disinterested in what their friend has to say. This may be demonstrated by ignoring, dismissing or talking over them. If you know a narcissist don't be fooled into thinking that the narcissist has a deep interest in your life because they are listening to you, they are just gathering their weapons for the potential war to come.

Training

◁╫──────◇─◦─◇──────╫▷

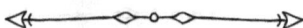

Although not specifically a word associated with narcissism, training is an important part of the arsenal. A narcissist will put a training operation in place when they form new relationships a with friend or members of a new family, such as in-laws. Typically they will idealise and use 'love bombing' techniques to draw in a new person. If you are the chosen target you will think this person is the best thing ever. Right from the start they have been there for you, been prepared to listen to your problems, been generous with their time, giving you gifts and really welcoming you into their family. They seem like the perfect new friend and you can't believe your good luck.

As you get to know them you begin to feel sorry for them as they tell you horrific stories about their crazy ex-friends and how they've had to cut them out of their lives, for the sake of their own mental health. They will list all the ways that they were harmed by these friends, they were too jealous, they never gave me space, they were always nagging me about my smoking. At this point you will be making mental notes never to behave like their terrible friends. They are training you to conform to their idea of friendship. To keep this wonderful person in your life you must never mention that they smoke too much. The more they tell you about past people's faults the more constrained you will become, forever checking yourself in case you too might become like the ex and be shunned. And you've seen how the shunning works, with family get togethers dominated by discussion of ex-friends and partners.

These are the people who say that they hate drama, but

in fact it's what keeps them going. Publicly they will talk about the toll it has brought and the stress that they suffer but in reality it is their life blood and if this particular drama goes away, although they will live off the stories forever, they will be searching for new battles. Life is all about competition and they are determined to win.

Triangulation

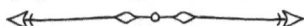

Triangulation, in psychological terms, is the use of a third party in a relationship in order to manipulate. Instead of communicating directly with their friend or family member, the narcissist will use a third person to relay information.

For example, if the narcissist's victims holds a different opinion which they want to undermine, they may recruit an unwitting third party to reinforce their own viewpoint. Often this additional person in the relationship is completely innocent and only believes that they are helping. The victim may feel overwhelmed by this two pronged attack and capitulate. This practice is not something employed in healthy relationships where the parties have direct communication and do not have to employ a third party to influence and act as messenger.

Another example is if a narcissist is having problems with someone who has seen through their subterfuge and glimpsed the real person behind the mask and they bring in a third party who is unaware of the situation to 'get them on side'. They will tell the third party how upset and stressed they are and who is the cause of all their problems. They will recite chapter and verse on how they have been tortured by this person and how they are trying to ruin their life. They will be convincing and taken at face value the third party will become their loyal supporter and either robustly defend the narcissist or refuse to have anything to do with the 'abuser'. The third party may go so far as to initiate hate campaigns on social networking sites and attack complete strangers just on the say so of a person they consider to be an upstanding member of the community. If they initiate an attack or jump to the defence of their friend, they will never hear the other side of the story and by the time they do, they will have been so indoctrinated that they won't believe a word that the victim has to say.

Word Salad

Word salad is an attractive term for a frustrating technique often used by narcissists to confuse and distract. The term itself originated to describe a form of speech adopted by people suffering from advanced schizophrenia or dementia when they may use a mixture of words and phrases that make sense individually but are used to construct sentences in a random and unintelligible manner. In terms of narcissism it is used to characterise a deliberate tactic used in arguments to deflect and baffle the listener.

If you argue with a narcissist you may find that after a few minutes you don't even know what you're talking about anymore. They will have twisted and turned the conversation every way until the origins have been lost in time. They will see this as a challenge that they must win, because how dare an inferior human being engage them in an argument or challenge them. If the narcissist feels themselves to be better educated and more articulate they will use this opportunity to demonstrate their superiority. They may confidently quote from academic studies to prove their point. The studies may be completely fabricated but they know their victim will have no knowledge of that and will not be motivated to follow it up because the narcissist is already onto their next ten points that will prove, beyond doubt, that they really didn't forget to put the bin out. Everything is a drama and they will spin the words around until their victim becomes too exhausted and confused to continue. The narcissist retires, happy to have won another argument, proving once again that they are the superior being.

Life is a Contest

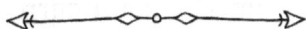

If you have a family member or friend who is a covert narcissist you may have sustained a relationship for years, even decades without realising that for the narcissist everything is about competition. They strive to win at all costs even if they self destruct in the process and an important part of their life is competing with you.

You may have been completely unaware that every interaction you had with them was being judged as they carefully weighed and measured which parts of their lives are superior to yours and which parts they need to improve upon. This will include all aspects of your life, for example; are your children more dysfunctional than theirs, are they more charitable than you, do they have a more fulfilling job, are they richer, do they live in a better area, do they have a better house, car, are they more educated? This competition even includes hobbies. If you take up a new interest it's likely that the narcissist will either take it up too and begin to seriously compete, or they will mock and belittle what you're doing as a complete waste of time. If they're not doing this openly they are very likely to be doing it behind your back.

Another revealing sign is that the narcissist will rarely recognise skills in others, unless it is so completely out of their zone as to be unattainable. For example, they may acknowledge that someone has a fabulous singing voice if they have never had any interest in singing themselves, however if it impinges in any way on their abilities they will either ignore it, dismiss it or belittle it. So, for example, a racing driver's skill might not be acknowledged because the narcissist drives a car and given the right circumstances they are sure that they could be world class and far superior to the current world champion.

There seems to be a presumption on the part of the narcissist that accolades given to another take away something from them. They imagine that there is a limited supply of praise and they don't want to give any away because this will diminish them as a person. It literally hurts them to give compliments.

It's likely that they won't acknowledge talent within their own family unless they are able to gain reflected glory or claim credit. So, for example, they may acknowledge their child's talent because the child obviously either inherited the skill from them, or they can claim credit for coaching. In this instance the child is just an extension of themselves.

If a friend shines in an area where they can't claim credit then they will do their best to dismiss and belittle them. They may do this in really obvious ways such as outright ignoring any discussion of the achievement and glossing over it in conversations. If pushed they may grudgingly nod and smile but afterwards in their own family group they will mock and degrade. Unbeknownst to you this is how your relationship is being judged and as long as the narcissist can feel that they are superior to you then everything, on the surface, will be fine. They will be feverishly comparing and contrasting and tallying up points and you will be completely oblivious, even imagining that you have a normal family relationship or friendship.

What you won't realise is that after every phone call or visit with the narcissist they will be bitching and complaining about any aspect of your life that seems to threaten their security. Within their own family group or friends they will be devaluing anything that appears to them to be superior but at this point they will still be able to maintain a relationship with you because they know, deep inside, that they are the better person with the superior life.

Then something happens to change the dynamic. The narcissist may become ill or lose their job and with their warped sense of self they begin to 'lose the game'. The only reason they ever maintained a relationship with you was to bolster their narcissistic supply - it made them feel good to be superior.

From your point of view and being oblivious to the workings of the narcissistic mind it's at precisely this moment that you are reaching out to them, offering help where you can. However, this is like a red rag to a bull to the wounded narcissist and it will be totally confusing to you as any offers of help are rejected without explanation and contact may even cease altogether as the narcissist withdraws. You may attempt to maintain communication with those around them but the narcissist may have instructed their immediate family and friends to reject any contact. The smear campaign may also have begun against you at this point in order to legitimise their rejection. Unknown to you they may even be accusing you of rejecting them in their hour of need.

If they can't invent a believable excuse to shun you then they may just say, darkly, that they have their reasons. This classic narcissistic mysteriousness works on two levels, it dissuades most people from enquiring further and also leads the enquirer to think that this must be something serious. It has to be something so bad that not only do they shun a member of their family but they can't even bring themselves to talk about it. In reality the narcissistic rage that they feel at no longer being 'the winner' has become overwhelming and it is easier to reject and forget you.

Illness

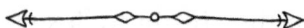

As we know, a narcissist likes to feel superior to others and sickness doesn't usually belong in that equation. So when a narcissist becomes ill they can feel diminished. If it is serious enough to effect their income and lifestyle they may go so far as to cut themselves off from friends and family because they feel humiliated. They don't want people to see them as weak and vulnerable. They may find it unbearable if their finances are diminished and it's impossible to live the life they feel they deserve. It is at this point that they may get into financial difficulties as they refuse to give up their lifestyle even though, for instance, they may no longer be working.

Instead they will be looking for a supply to bolster their finances, maybe sending other family members out to work or moving in with a parent or sibling. In their own way of thinking they have lost all of their kudos with their friends and extended family, given that their main goal and interest in life was to brag about their lifestyle and money. Now they feel they have nothing, because their whole self worth depends on achievement and status. They will have dropped friends or family in the past who fail to live up to their expectations or achievements, so becoming sick themselves and unable to keep up their self defined standards will make them unhappy. An unhappy narcissist is not a good person to be around.

The narcissist conversely may have another reaction to illness. If it is serious it may be their narcissistic dream come true. Now everyone has to be good to them, nobody can talk about them behind their back (paranoia makes them think that everyone is talking about them, all the time) and they can get people to do whatever they want very easily indeed. They may exaggerate the seriousness of their ailment once they see the effectiveness of using it as a tool. They will post on social media about it constantly and it will almost become a career. They may become an expert on this particular disease and write long articles about the problems. They may join and then try to take over a group dedicated to the illness. They will have the worst or most unusual case ever known, of course.

At the extreme edge, we have the narcissist faker who sees what an effective tool a serious illness can be and outrageously lies that they have terminal cancer or another life threatening disease in order to manipulate friends and strangers. This generally only works with people who are not too close to the narcissist although it's not unknown for a narcissist to even fool a partner into thinking they have a serious illness in order that they won't leave them, or will pander to their needs. Who can refuse someone who's dying?

More commonly though, the narcissist will fake something less dramatic and crucially something that can't be proven one way or the other. Debilitating back pain, excruciating migraines or clinical depression are all targets for the narcissist. This type of disability is typically not provable or testable and the narcissist may research the most suitable illness for their needs. For example, they don't want to work but still want to be able to tend to their garden. So maybe depression would be better than back pain? As unbelievable as this sounds this is how some narcissists work. The stress/depression type of illness can work on many different levels of manipulation. They can gradually manoeuvre their family/friends into a state where they have to be 'careful' around them. They mustn't have any stress and people will be careful with them because of their 'condition'. We can see how, for a narcissist, this will be huge advantage in their bigger game. Naturally it won't effect anything that they really want to do and the depression will come and go depending on their schedule. It's the perfect example to get out of their responsibilities when they would prefer a 'duvet' day. They will post memes on social media about how people should recognise and support people with mental health issues. Surprisingly though, they don't have much sympathy for other people who are genuinely sick. They will often accuse them of feigning illness because as a narcissist, at some level they believe everyone is as devious as they are and they are always eager to 'out' people.

The breathtaking hypocrisy of what they are doing is never even considered. They manage to convince themselves that their actions are different because, of course, they have the justification that they shouldn't have to work because they are special, while others are lazy fakers. They are genuine and would be outraged if you even hinted that they were faking. Remarkably though they can shake off their ailments when there is something they really want to do, like go to a party or on holiday. The only time during this period that their disability will reoccur is if they are asked to carry heavy suitcases!

If a narcissist is confronted for their bad behaviour they may use illness as one of their back up arguments. "Did you even know how sick I was? You didn't even care. I nearly DIED!" This is the perfect distraction. If they can't actually use a particular illness for the period in question the will happily use their old standby, stress. Stress can cover a multitude of sins.

Of course I'm not saying that those of us who suffers from anxiety, clinical depression, migraines or back problems are all faking our illnesses. However, the narcissist will research an illness to find one that genuine sufferers have problems 'proving', both to friends, families and benefit authorities and jump on the coat tails of these 'unprovable' illnesses . A narcissist's search engine history can make for interesting reading, although most will have learnt to expunge search history early on in their 'career'. Trying to catch a narcissist out sometimes feels like being a detective and if you've reached the point where you are searching and watching, then you are almost certainly living with someone who is suffering from this type of personality disorder.

Money

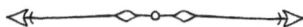

Narcissists usually want money badly but generally they don't want to have to work to get it. When they have money they often spend it recklessly, if they don't have it they may run up debts or spend other people's money.

It has been said that in the last forty years the ability to obtain easy credit has enabled narcissists. With credit we can appear to be wealthier than we are in reality. Narcissists use credit as a boost for a fake social status that enables them to fool their victims. The narcissistic nature is to boast about money and possessions in order to gain narcissist supply. They are superior to others and any good fortune that comes their way will be broadcast far and wide so that their fans can congratulate them on their well deserved success.

Broadcasting can be accomplished under many different guises and a covert narcissist will often communicate it in a suitably humble or subtle way, for example taking a selfie but making sure that their beautiful new possession can be seen 'accidentally' in the background. In addition, narcissists are often masters of the humblebrag when using social media. This is the art of telling the world how great your life is under the guise of a self deprecating comment or a complaint. For example they may make statements such as, 'Wow, I can't believe I looked so fat when I was interviewed on TV yesterday' or 'I hate looking so young, I'm always being asked for ID when I just want a drink! #Annoying'. Research suggests that this method of bragging is easily detected by the intended audience and intensely disliked. However, the counter productive nature of the technique is lost on the self absorbed narcissist.

Because of the narcissist's irresponsibility with money there will be many periods in his or her life when they are broke. We may assume that a narcissist would be too proud to announce this to the world however, on the contrary, when they start to panic about their lack of money and status they may begin to post about it on their social media feed, albeit in a suitably subtle way. Maybe they will tell tales of unexpected incidents that have left them without money for something they had been planning. It was their dream, but now it's been dashed and it wasn't their fault! This is done in the hope of eliciting sympathy from their followers who may then offer them cash. Of course if this happens publicly they will protest that this was not the intention of their post, but they will accept it, reluctantly. They couldn't possibly insult the donor by refusing. They will be secretly hoping a GoFundMe page is started, likewise they will accept the cash, under much fake protest.

The root of this behaviour is entitlement. Because they are so special they expect to be funded throughout their lives. They don't expect to have to work like inferior people, they are too good for that. So they will go from family handouts to begging on social media and in their old age they will return to family members expecting them to take care of them, both physically and financially.

The narcissist's social media feed is a strange mix of humble-bragging about their good fortune and humble-begging hoping that people will help them. Should you loan money to a narcissist? Will they ever pay you back? That depends.

If they get more narcissistic supply from paying it back they will. It is also worth bearing in mind that they may be coldly setting up a scenario for the future, for example, borrow a small amount, pay it back promptly so they will be trusted with a larger amount later that they have no intention of ever paying back.

If they don't honour the loan they will always be able to justify and rationalise their action. They may feel entitled to keep the money you loaned them because they have done so much for you in the past and this is payback. Or if they think you have more money than you deserve then it's perfectly fair, in their mind, for you to give a portion of it to them. Alternatively, they may feel you have done them wrong with some slight, real or imagined. Your punishment for the crime is for them to never repay you. If you ask them when you are likely to get your money back, no matter how gently and tactfully, they will be outraged and quickly adopt the well-used victim persona. How dare you demand money from them when they are in such an appalling situation in their life. Don't you realise how stressed they are and you're just making things worse? An example of this attitude is the indignant letter in response to a gentle enquiry regarding the repayment of a loan, impatiently asserting that they'll deal with the matter when they've returned from their Caribbean holiday! If you persist with your intention to be repaid you will be met with an abusive and out of proportion reaction and YOU will quickly turn out to be the cause of all their pain. If the narcissist realises, at this point, that they might actually have to pay back the loan they may begin the devalue and discard. In their own warped sense of reality it is better to lose a family member or friend than to have to pay back money to which they feel morally entitled.

The narcissist and responsibility

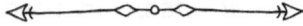

Narcissists are experts at shirking responsibility. They want to live their lives exactly as they choose without hindrance and the day to day chores that burden lesser people. If they don't have a rewarding job then they won't work. They will find other ways to support themselves, possibly crime or, more likely, getting people around them to work and support them. They will have a million plausible excuses not to do something that makes them feel even slightly uncomfortable or that doesn't fit in with their plans.

To maintain their public image they may initially agree to almost any request to help. For example, if there is a volunteering opportunity they will never say no when asked to give their time. Always the first to offer but strangely when it comes to the day something will have happened. They will have car trouble, they unexpectedly have to cover child care for a relative or their aforementioned illness returns to lay them low. Most of the time these reasons will be real and they will have gone to great lengths to manufacture them . Their excuse will be watertight so they will be maintaining their reputation as being the salt of the earth, pillar of the community type. That perception will be in people's minds even though they do little of the work they agree to. In fact, for a while at least, they end up with a better reputation than the person who said no initially but stepped in at the last minute after the narcissist pulled out.

Public image and reputation is the most important

aspect of life for many narcissists and they will perform all sorts of tricks and deceits to make sure that they are thought of in a good light even if it is below them to do any of the actual work.

A covert narcissist often doesn't want to socialise, unless there's something in it for them. If this is a way to climb the social ladder, they can make a valuable contact or they are looking for a new source of supply then it's acceptable. However, as a way of spending their free time they find social gatherings boring. They don't have a genuine interest in other people, who of course, are their inferiors. They find the whole idea of making small talk in a pub or bar tiresome. It only becomes attractive if they become the centre of attention and can hold court with their opinions. They don't like to listen to others and will quickly shut down any competitor for attention. So unless that is the scenario they will make excuses not to interact with people. They know that they are unable to make genuine connections with other people and they don't want to spend an evening being reminded of how separate they are from the rest of humanity.

Creating Drama

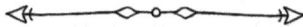

Phrases such as "I hate drama". "You are entering a No Drama Zone"' are often bandied about by narcissists. They proclaim to want nothing to do with drama - they can't deal with the stress - but their lives are full of the drama that they claim to abhor. They just want a quiet life and it's not their fault. It's like the cartoon of the bad driver who is boasting that he's never had an accident in his life, but all the cars around him are crashing because of his lack of driving skills. He drives away unscathed and oblivious.

The covert narcissist however, is not oblivious. Their strategy is to cause as many crashes as they can but still appear to be the innocent party. According to them it must be coincidence that the people they get mixed up with are crazy. When this 'coincidence' starts to become obvious they will emphasise all the good relationships they have. Everyone else in their family is just fine, thank you. The relationships that they hold up for inspection, however, are the ones they control in their bubble of close family and friends. They conveniently ignore the others they have shunned or who have dropped them over the years. They are no longer relevant.

The elimination of the past gets easier for the narcissist as they age and people who inconveniently know the truth about their dysfunctional relationships die. They can create a clean slate with every death. The narcissist may not genuinely be touched by the death of any family member, but they will quickly start to work out how this rubbing out of inconvenient memories can be used to their advantage as they work on reinventing themselves for each new audience.

After their parents have died, for instance, they may begin talking about their terrible childhood when there is nobody around to contradict their version of events. The narcissist is taking advantage of being the last family member standing, or they have managed to build up a reputation where their stories are believed without question and others have been silenced. A narcissist is tenacious and family members may get tired of constantly having to dispute the tall tales that the narcissist spins. It may just be easier to let the lies sit there. As long as it's not directly attacking them it may cause less stress to let the the narcissist carry on with the sob stories about their terrible childhood. The narcissist may have had a relatively wealthy, privileged and loving background but they will always be able to spin it from the angle of being a victim. Often they will say they have triumphed despite this adversity and they will use the past to accentuate any small achievement in the present by contrasting it with their poor/uneducated/abused early years.

People who know the truth may be suffering from 'putting the record straight' fatigue. You can imagine if this has continued for several years and you are met with disbelief from the narcissist's group of friends and you are then accused of lying yourself. After a while you give up. Why on earth would you pull that kind of hassle onto yourself? So if the narcissist is just lying to bolster his own popularity eventually the family member who is able to dispute his version of events will just ignore him. Emotionally healthy people do their best not to constantly engage in disputes and conflicts.

So the covert narcissist, in all their feigned innocence, will sail through life drama-free as their friends and family crash in flames around him. However, behind each trauma there is the narcissist whispering and stirring the pot. It never appears to be malicious gossip because the covert narcissist has trained, sometimes over many years, to stir up situations and at the same time make themselves the victim.

If a narcissist is a new contact they may confide in you about someone who is treating them badly. You may feel flattered at this level of trust because you've only just met. You will be appalled at the nature of the abuse that this person is suffering. Of course, you are only hearing one side of the story. It may be that the narcissist's enemy is reacting to being taunted and goaded, but this will have been carefully edited out of the narrative. You will be told that this person is mentally unstable and that the narcissist is being targeted, totally unfairly. They may begin to hint that this person has insulted you too. For normal emotionally healthy people their goal is to draw their friends and family together, engendering trust and love but for the narcissist it is completely the opposite. They live for confusion and discord as they sit back and enjoy the view. Nero fiddling while Rome burns.

Talking to a narcissist

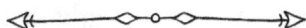

Talking to a narcissist may be a misnomer. They generally love the sound of their own voices and you may find you are being talked at rather than having an actual conversation. If you do manage to find a gap and submit your own thoughts, they may act obviously bored because if the focus of what you're saying is not about them they have an extremely short attention span.

Many narcissists actively enjoy arguing and often believe that they are particularly skilled in this area. They may even provoke disputes if they feel that life is boring and/or running too smoothly. A narcissist may become uneasy if there is no conflict in their lives - they prefer to be causing chaos and confusion and they don't want their victim to feel complacent and comfortable.

As in many other areas of life they see debate as a competition they have to win. Their aim is to manipulate and control you and they will use whatever techniques they need to in order to achieve success. This may include constant interruption, lying, pretending they didn't hear you and punishing you with silence if you're threatening to gain the upper hand. They will look for ways that you have insulted them and if they can't find any they will invent them. In this case they are able to become the victim and turn the focus to themselves.

So just for their own amusement and as an opportunity to flex their narcissistic muscle they may exaggerate, twist words or simply tell lies. For example they may say that they've heard that a member of your family has been criticising you and watch to gauge your reaction. If you react emotionally they will stay calm and criticise you for the way you're responding. They may play devil's advocate, just for fun, and comment that maybe the relative criticising you has a point. If this triggers an angry outburst they will smirk, roll their eyes and use condescending and patronising language. Then they will show faux concern about how easily upset you are, how over-sensitive and how they are beginning to become concerned about your mental health.

The staged and controlled argument can be used as a device to accomplish anything from an excuse to avoid an event or family gathering to the beginning stage of a devalue and discard. Everything about this is your fault because you are so unstable. A narcissist will use words in an argument to distract and deflect. This may include the use of circular arguments, ie just when you think you have a point resolved they will bring it up again and again as though the initial conversation never happened. They may also switch personas, alternating between screaming and shouting to quiet and thoughtful. Bad cop/good cop in one body. Word salad, mentioned previously, is also a technique used to confuse their victim.

Even though we are led to believe, usually by the narcissist themselves, that they are of superior intelligence they will often resort to scraping the bottom of the barrel when it comes to arguments. If they find they can no longer manipulate your opinions and emotions they may resort to inappropriate jokes, mocking and name calling. A quick and lazy way to degrade a well informed and carefully researched argument is to call the opponent 'a baby' or a 'special snowflake' and claim that their opinions are idiotic or stupid. Instead of forming a convincing counter argument, the narcissist may go on to attack the personality or appearance of their opponent in an attempt to sabotage their self-esteem and diminish their credibility. They may draw attention to a feature that they find objectionable or ugly. Often this is a direct projection of their own insecurities, for example a narcissist who is overweight may call their victim fat and somehow will be completely blind to the hypocrisy.

The techniques that a narcissist uses in arguments can be exhausting and people who are close, such as family members often fall into one of two groups. The first are the enablers who agree with everything. The narcissist can do or say no wrong and the enablers are steadfastly in agreement with everything they say or do. No need for arguments. Just agree. The second group are those who bite their tongue. They might not agree with the narcissist but they know better than to actively disagree. They have experienced arguments that can go on for hours or days and witnessed the insults, word salad, sulking and temper tantrums that, in the end, do not amount to resolution. They have learnt that it is better to just stay quiet, displaying tacit agreement. Anything for a quiet life.

Black and white and the perfect self image.

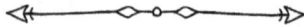

The narcissist seems to believe that everyone either has or should have the same morals and standards as themselves. They have this high ideal of themselves, their imagined self, their idea of the perfect person. Of course the reality is somewhat different but whenever they transgress from this ideal self image they are able to justify and excuse it. They will talk themselves into finding a reason why they shoplifted, or why they cheated on their partner and it will usually be somebody else's fault, so they can relax with the idea that it's really nothing to do with them and all about outside influences.

However, if someone else commits the same crime then there is no such benefit of the doubt given. Their thinking is black and white and seems to get more entrenched the older they get. For example, one couple set high standards for their family. Although ordinary working class people their family, they believed, were on a level above their neighbours and friends. Their family had morals. They were strict with their kids and they themselves were upright models of society with kids to be proud of. When the narcissist found out that his son's girlfriend was pregnant, he was incredibly and inappropriately angry. How could their son have let their family down in this way? The anger subsided eventually to be replaced with shame. This was evident when the family delayed telling anyone in their extended family or friends about the pregnancy for months. When the narcissist eventually told his friends about it, he displayed embarrassment, which his friends couldn't understand because their children had also had babies 'out of wedlock'. What did it matter as long as the boy was accepting responsibility and stepping up to fatherhood? But it was different for the narcissist, he and his family were superior to all these lesser people and now, in his eyes, he had been dragged down to their level by the behaviour of his son.

The narcissist's blinkered self focus seems reluctant to accept that other people have different values, ideas and even hobbies. This is reminiscent of the idealisation phase of the romantic narcissist and it also appears to spill over into the family/friend relationship. The narcissist makes a new friend and really admires everything about them, but then discovers that they're not a fan of the particular TV series that the narcissist enjoys. Of course, on the surface, they accept this in the friend but deep down it takes away something from the relationship. The friend is no longer the 'perfect' friend that he once was. Behind his back the friend may begin to be devalued when the narcissist gets together with his own family. "Bill's okay, but I can't understand why he hates Breaking Bad. He is weird though." There is an unrealistic notion of friendship where the friend has to agree and be interested in everything that the narcissist is or they are relegated down the pecking order of importance. They can't be a real friend if they are not a mirror image of the narcissist.

Nasty nicknames

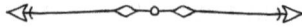

Narcissists will often have nicknames for every person they come into contact with including friends, colleagues and members of their own families. These will not usually be affectionate pet names but rather derogatory descriptions using appearance or behaviour to belittle and dehumanise friends or family members. Sometimes this bullying tactic will be used openly to humiliate their victims in front of others, which is often the case with the narcissistic parent.

"Oh here comes Stuttery Sue", might be used to greet their child who suffers with a speech impediment. Anything that they deem to be imperfect about their child will be used to humiliate them. If they are challenged they will resort to the usual, "it's just a joke" and "you're too sensitive" defence.

A covert narcissist, who doesn't want to risk being confronted, may only share their name-calling of adults with a select group of enablers, often close family. This practice is an attempt to dehumanise their friends and acquaintances, making them the butt of private jokes and enabling the narcissist to feel superior.

80 | Viper

Crazy making behaviour

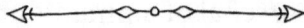

If someone tells us they are suffering from narcissistic abuse our first instinct may be disbelief because the alleged abuser is such a 'nice' person. Typically abusers appear to be 'better' people than their victims. Calmer, more tolerant, charming and generally more interesting. By the time the victim is at the point where they can articulate the abuse, they may have become incoherent with anger and want to obsessively talk about what has happened to them. When they are put into words the incidents may seem superficial and petty. It can be confusing to hear these stories because they might not make sense and the victim may appear to be mentally unstable. This is all part of the game for the covert narcissist.

Covert narcissists are said to be extremely clever but in my experience this expertise is demonstrated primarily in one area. Manipulation. When abusing people they will do so in ways that can never be fully uncovered, or at least if someone dares to break cover and tell the story of the abuse, it will appear to be so inconsequential as not to warrant an explanation. If they are confronted they will be able to explain it away easily, they didn't mean it like that, they were misunderstood, misquoted, they weren't talking about the victim and we may be left wondering why the victim is so upset for little apparent reason, leading to the logical conclusion that they are suffering from some kind of mental breakdown. The victim is then re-victimised, and anything they say is treated with a degree of scepticism. This is a wonderful result for the narcissist. They can wear their victim/martyr status with pride. "I have done everything for her and look how she repays me". The fake tears will barely hide the huge grin as they are handed an arsenal of ammunition.

The narcissist is now able to publicise what has happened, both in real life and on social media, ie they have been accused of being a horrible person and of course, as you all know they are a wonderful human being. Not only does this vindicate them against all past accusations but inoculates them against any blame for future abuse. They will have a burning desire to punish this person who dared to disagree or challenge them and now they have the advantage of their victim not being believed. In addition they can now play the stress card . Any promise they want to break they can do with impunity and publicly because everyone will understand the great stress that has been caused by the victim. Can you imagine if this was a case of physical abuse, the person with the black eye is shunned and the one who punched them is lauded as the poor long suffering victim.

As we can see, if the victim of narcissistic abuse isn't suffering from mental instability before their encounter with the narcissist, then it is likely they will be after living in the upside down, back to front world of a narcissist. If they knew they were dealing with a narcissist before exposing them it might have taken them a long time to pluck up courage before revealing the abuse. Now they have become the crazy abuser; nothing they say will ever be believed by the abuser's group. The more they protest and try to show proof of their abuse the more deranged they appear. Meanwhile the narcissist watches and smirks.

Diversion tactics

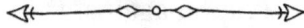

D iversion tactics are used by narcissists to silence and confuse their victims often in order to take the attention away from their wrong doing. For example, if you ask a narcissist family member a direct question such as why they didn't invite you to their wedding, they may answer that they're sorry about that but life has been very complicated for them and they can't really go into details. This statement achieves several objectives. First of all the apology or more accurately the fake apology. This takes the wind out of your sails, even an insincere apology is difficult not to acknowledge. Secondly, you have to feel sorry for them, they are obviously the victim of some kind of trauma, a trauma so bad they can't even bring themselves to talk about it. Any further questioning would be insensitive, wouldn't it? As they realise that you are a sensitive person they are counting on you to just accept what they say and never mention it again. Successful distraction. It's time to get used to the idea that a narcissist will always experience life in a more intense way than you will and whatever your pain, theirs will be worse. Finally, even though it comes with an apology the narcissist is clearly stating that they are dismissing you as not important enough to be part of their inner circle.

A narcissist may use shame to control a victim and divert attention away from the real issue. They have no hesitation in using traumas that have happened in their victim's past to re-victimise them. They may imply that the traumatic event must have been in the victim's fault, in a less than obvious way. They will do this to make the victim feel ashamed and they will use anything that the victim has shared with them about their past as a weapon against them, especially if they are beginning to challenge the narcissist's power and/or call them out about their bad behaviour.

In a family situation when a narcissist has discarded a member the shunning might not be the end of the relationship. Their obsessive nature and desire to 'finish off' the victim with their 'win at all costs' mentality may see them driven to distract attention away from any aspect of life in which their victim is successful. For example, if the victim is a violinist, the narcissist may take violin lessons. Money may be no object as they obsessively need to prove themselves the more talented violinist and they will put all of their energy and time into this pursuit in order to prove themselves 'better' than their victim. They will exaggerate every achievement and they will be ready with their social media machine to tell the world about their accolades. They will go out of their way to make sure their victim knows as much about it as possible. "See, I'm better than you at everything", is the message and they can, once again, have their self esteem boosted and superiority confirmed by external sources. If they are not capable of outperforming their victim themselves they may encourage a close member of their group, preferably another family member, to learn to play the violin. They can then wield the achievements of this family member as a weapon in the battle for supremacy.

Another form of diversionary tactic is to invent faux concern about their victim's mental health. They will express mock sadness at how their victim is bi-polar, or suffers with depression and how this has made them unpredictable and unreliable. All those medications that they take, oh dear. However, they still continue to taunt and bully a person they believe is suffering from mental health issues and use inappropriate language to describe someone with mental health issues. Of course they say that they only do it because they are provoked and what they are doing is:

a) completely justified

or

b) it's only a light-hearted joke

c) the victim is too sensitive - a snowflake

d) actually they're not even talking about them. They could be talking about anyone.

Choose any of the above!

If you challenge a narcissist about anything they may simply change the subject. For example you may ask why they didn't pick up the milk on their way home and they may ignore it and tell you a story about the drama that happened at work. If you come back to the missing milk they may say that you 'always' spoil their stories, and are 'never' satisfied. You didn't even notice that they put the bin out this morning. If they are a narcissistic parent they may start talking about your childhood and how you were never able to appreciate everything that they did for you and you always have to criticise them for the smallest transgression. You are damaging their self esteem and it's no wonder they're so unhappy. You know you're in trouble when they begin a sentence with "What about that time when you.. " It has no relevance to what you're discussing at that moment but it's a way of distracting you if you fall into the carefully laid trap of defending actions that took place years earlier. Again they manage to make themselves into the victim, the episode may end in tears or with them storming out and if you are able to wade through the thick fog of diversion you may wonder how all this came about just because you asked where is the milk. If you're further able to analyse the situation you may wonder how and why they are able to put so much energy into diverting from such a simple, everyday problem. It would have been so much easier to say, oops sorry I'll pop out and get some. Of course that would be admitting that they have human frailties just like everyone else and as we know by now the narcissist works on a whole different level. Challenging and debating with a narcissist is like that proverbial occupation, herding cats.

On a broader level it is reminiscent of political discussions when a party is accused of some heinous act and the response of their supporters might be, "Well what about the other party, they haven't always been squeaky clean.?" The use of 'whataboutery' is an obvious and immature arguing tactic designed to derail discussions. It is a way of responding to criticism by accusing your opponent of similar or worse faults and is a distraction technique that is often favoured by the narcissist.

A covert narcissist will propagandise us to believe that they are the target of abuse. They will be ostentatious victims, openly talking about the persecution they have suffered at the hands of their torturer and repeatedly signalling their vulnerability. This is an echo chamber of insanity where the covert narcissist will take the moral high ground. They will try to pre-empt their victims attempts to get help by accusing them of the words and actions that they are using themselves. Even more crazy-making is if the victim outs them as a narcissist, they will research narcissism and then tell their group of enablers that the victim is projecting. They are the real victim here. You can see that a casual observer to this situation may throw their hands up, saying, "I can't cope with this" and walk away. The narcissist's loyal followers will stay true however and re-victimise the accuser. Victims who begin to defend themselves appear guilty almost by default. As they begin to offer explanations we naturally judge them on how plausible they are. We generally don't question why they have been accused in the first place.

It is almost inevitable that when a narcissist's victim begins to speak out they become the target of even more insidious abuse. They have educated themselves, they know exactly what is going on but they can't prove it to others, and in fact they are now being thought of as narcissists themselves. Mental instability is often the outcome of this scenario which, of course, proves the narcissist's point.

"I told you she was crazy, here's the proof". In situations like this the narcissist is often able to fool authorities such as the police, lawyers, social workers and psychiatrists. All can be sucked in to the topsy turvy world of the narcissist.

For many narcissists their whole lives are focussed on winning, no matter what the cost, and they will never give up. They will tenaciously track down 'evidence' to prove every point they have ever made. They will obsessively scour social media platforms for anything to support their case, taking screenshots and even manipulating those screenshots e.g., changing the date so it appears that this particular post wasn't in response to their provocation, it happened days before. They will hide anything they have said that exposes their guilt by deleting posts, but also using other means to pass messages onto their victims like making accounts in false names or having a discussion denigrating their victims on a friend's account. This has the advantage that it is not visible to their own group of friends so they can be more openly hostile without drawing any suspicion from their carefully nurtured group.

Hypocrisy

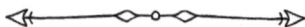

For all that is said about narcissists, and covert narcissists in particular, being clever, it is amazing that they can be so lacking in self awareness. When a narcissist rants about the actions of others, they are often carrying out the same actions themselves and may be doing so in a very public manner but are somehow blind to the similarities. We sometimes see this being demonstrated in their online behaviour. One of the most blatant examples I have experienced is witnessing a narcissist cyber stalking a victim, obsessively checking their victim's website on an hourly basis all through the night and then complaining, loudly and publicly on a social media platform that their victim is always watching them. They may call out their target publicly with 'proof' that they are watching them, but don't seem to realise that they would only have access to that information if they themselves had been constantly checking their victim's social media page. If challenged, however, they will be able to justify, to their own satisfaction at least, why their stalking is different. They will almost certainly have a high minded or wordy explanation. Maybe they will be gathering evidence in preparation for a criminal court case or maybe they're working undercover for MI5. The more they are cornered with proof of their hypocrisy the more outlandish their explanations will become.

In a family situation this sort of hypocrisy seems to be

replicated across generations. A child might criticise a parent for feuding with relatives but when they become adults they replicate the identical behaviour. If you point it out to them they will go to great lengths to tell you that this is different. It is interesting to speculate that if social media had been available fifty years ago we might have seen the same behaviour laid out in black and white and it is a sobering thought to imagine that in fifty years time, this will still be happening, each generation brainwashed by the narcissistic family.

Jealousy

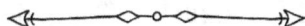

Pathological jealousy is at the root of many malignant and destructive behaviours perpetrated by a narcissist. Although they may be devoid of many emotions unfortunately jealousy is not one of them. Social status and wealth are the most obvious sources of jealousy and the narcissist's heightened sense of entitlement drives them to be recognised as the best, the most famous and always the centre of attention.

A narcissist is envious of almost everyone, in all strands of life whether that is a neighbour, friend or member of their own family, and they will get immense pleasure from sabotaging and undermining those that they envy in order to shore up their false sense of superiority. If something good is happening in the victim's life their jealousy will dictate that they have to 'bring them down a peg or two', they can't have them being the centre of attention and taking the light away from them. They may accuse the victim of being arrogant or boastful if they present their achievement with a healthy belief in themselves.

Narcissists behave as if there is a limited amount of love and attention in the world and they deserve it all. Success or achievement by others diminishes their own achievements, so they have to go out of their way to minimise the successes of others in order to bolster their self esteem. Many narcissists have an insatiable appetite for the luxuries in life such as expensive cars, an impressive house and exotic holidays and they will be relentless in their drive to acquire them no matter what the cost. Although many of us have similar desires it is the narcissist who will rarely use the conventional method of working to obtain life's luxuries. They devise other ways of obtaining money and that might be borrowing from friends and family or getting into debt. They can appear to have no boundaries with regards to debt and their desire to outdo their friends and family with the best car or newest gadget seemingly overrides financial acumen.

They will go out on a whim and purchase a new sofa on a credit card when they know there will be no money coming in. "It's okay", they say, "the payments don't start for a year" and their optimism for the future will override any concern that they can't really afford the purchase. They have the idea that in a year's time their grand plan will have come to fruition or something or someone else may turn up and pay their way.

Narcissists have an overwhelming desire to be admired and the type of narcissist determines the items that they need to acquire to achieve that, at least in their own mind. It might be a new purchase to make their home superior to their friends, they might need to move house to show that they are moving up in the world, or a showcase holiday in order to display their affluence on Instagram. A cerebral narcissist might need a qualification to demonstrate their superior intelligence. A somatic narcissist might desire a six pack to show off their fabulous body. If they can check these items off their list, it will temporary calm the monstrous envy they feel of friends and family members.

Monstrous is not an exaggeration. They almost feel physical pain if a friend or relative is achieving. It is irrelevant to the narcissist if the reward has been earned by hard work. This person, inferior to them, is still not worthy. On the face of it and in public view they will often appear happy that a family member has been awarded a degree or got a fabulous new job, but inside they will be seething. They have learnt that displaying jealousy openly is not an attractive trait but at home, with their closest malignant enablers they will talk down the person who they believe is belittling them by their achievements. In private, with their closest friends, they will become a pompous critic in order to undermine other's achievements and undertakings.

Depending on the degree of enabling available they may openly trash the person and degrade their achievement by saying, for example, that they didn't get the job fairly, or that the job is not all that and discuss the disadvantages of it at length, ad nauseam and finally conclude that despite the money/perks/status it's not a job they would want themselves. This self soothing will calm the green monster for a while and reassure them that the situation is all good. The job is garbage, why would they want it and their relative is dumb for taking it. Phew! Everyone feels okay now.

If they really are unable to do that, ie the job really is THAT good and they can't find anything negative to turn it around they will be eaten up by jealousy and become extremely unpleasant to live with until they can find something that will outperform the achievement. It doesn't have to be anything that in reality is better than their relative's job, just something in their own mind, that they can justify is more important. It will often be the exact opposite of their relation's achievement. For example, if the job is all about money and status then our narcissist will be extolling the virtues of the simple life. They will be telling us that the best things in life are free. In that moment they will actually believe what they are saying because they are using this charade to calm the jealous monster that is threatening to eat them alive. Emotionally healthy people do not have to sabotage, undermine and belittle other people's achievements. The first reaction to seeing somebody else happy and excited about something they have achieved is not to lash out, or plot and plan their demise.

As jealous as the narcissist is of almost everyone they also believe that everyone is jealous of them; their lifestyle, home, family, car, whatever. If it 'belongs' to them it must be the best and of course everyone would want what they have. If they are publicly called out on their narcissistic behaviour in any way when they begin the devalue and discard phase of a relationship, one of the shots in the smear campaign is that they will tell people that the victim is jealous of them or their family. They expect that this will convince everyone because of course, their lifestyle is something that anyone would be envious of, so for their victim to be angry with them the obvious assumption is that the root cause is jealousy.

Running in alignment with the jealousy narcissists are usually highly competitive and will behave badly in any kind of competition. They are the adults who cheat at board games and have tantrums or sulk when they don't win. They can't bear to lose at anything.

Justification

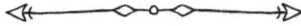

The narcissist is never accountable and can justify any kind of behaviour, sometimes with the most outrageous explanations. In fact the more monstrous the behaviour, the more surreal the excuses become. They are adept at distraction, so for example if you catch them stealing money from your purse, they will tell you that they thought that's where you kept your aspirin and they've got the most awful headache. The money in their hand? They were just moving it out of the way to see if the aspirin had slipped to the bottom. But really, this headache is so appalling and they think it started when you were vacuuming. That vacuum cleaner is just so noisy, it can't be good for anyone's health to be bombarded with that sort of noise. Do you think we should do some research to see if we can find a vacuum cleaner to buy based on its decibel level?

You get the idea? We have gone from stealing to buying a new vacuum without missing a beat and it will have been done so smoothly, without a stutter or a flushed face. It is likely we will have been convinced, and we may even feel a little guilty, first at having thought they were stealing and secondly that it was probably our fault they had a headache in the first place. The narcissist will be laughing at our gullibility and this will be a further sign, to them, of how much more intelligent they are than any 'normal' person.

No matter what happens to them they will be able to justify it. If they've lost a job it will never be their fault. Even if the reason they got fired was because they were too lazy to get out of bed in the morning, they will come up with an excuse about the work being so tiring or stressful that they couldn't help but oversleep in the morning.

The violent narcissist, will use the ever popular justification 'you made me do it' after they have physically lashed out, blaming the victim for their own lack of control.

During the last few years true crime drama has become popular on television. I'm referring to the ones that follow the criminal from their capture, through their arrest and to the eventual outcome at their trial. We are now able to see the interviews that take place with police as it happened. Many suspects take the 'no comment' route to avoid incriminating themselves, but occasionally you will see a suspect so confident in his ability to fool the police they will give chapter and verse on their excuses, justifications and alibis. Sometimes they are such obvious lies that they look like the reasonings of a 4 year old who has eaten the cake, has icing all over his face and is trying to explain that he didn't eat any of the cake at all. In the interview room the suspect will justify everything about his actions, for example he had a baseball bat on him because he was going to practice his swing at the park.

" Yes, at 10pm, its a good time of day to practice, it's quiet."

" So where's the ball?"

"Oh I leave the ball at the park, I have a hiding place for it."

"So we will be able to find it?"

"No, well actually a dog stole it from me last night and ran off. I was just coming home when this all happened."

"What about the blood on the baseball bat."

"Yes, when I found the beaten man and tried to give him CPR, I knelt down beside him and I must have put the bat down in the blood."

The more he is questioned the more he has an answer for everything and we may even see him smirking as he thinks he so much more intelligent than the stupid policeman. As witnesses to this we can see almost immediately that what he's saying makes no sense at all and it becomes very obvious that he's lying.

The classic covert narcissist will be used to operating in their own bubble where they have carefully trained the people around them to conform to expectations. It is often when they have to perform in a public arena without their 'support team' that they begin to unravel and everyone suddenly sees the narcissist for what they are.

Movies and pets

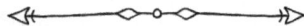

There is a question that is raised occasionally when people believe that someone can't be a narcissist because they cry at sad films.

"Even when they don't have an audience, I've caught them crying. Doesn't that prove they can't be a narcissist?"

There are several theories about narcissists crying at sad movies. One is that they are crying for themselves. But isn't that empathy? When we can put ourselves into the place of someone else and feel their emotions? However, this type of crying may be nothing to do with empathy. This is a narcissist being reminded that the level of emotion being portrayed on the screen is something that they will never experience in their real lives. These are tears of self pity and grief for their emotionless and empty inner life.

Sometimes a self-aware narcissist will say that the emotions in a movie are much clearer and cleaner, easy to understand. A movie director will be skilled in merging this combination of words, images and music for a particular effect and most of us will cry at the point he has prescribed, including the narcissist.

Of course the other scenario is that it's an act. Narcissists are often good at being able to cry at will, it's a learned skill and can help them get out of difficult situations. If they have been caught out and they need to gather their excuses and justifications, they can burst into tears for a few moments which can work as an effective distraction mechanism. The nature of narcissism is that the sufferers of this personality disorder are empty with no genuine feelings for other people, so they really are not capable of empathy for others. They may however, put on a display of emotions to persuade the person they are with, or who might be entering the room any moment, that they really are a sensitive and caring individual.

So what about animals? You may feel that the narcissist you know loves animals. Doesn't that prove that they have feelings and are a 'good' person? It's questionable that the narcissist 'loves' animals. They may find the emotionally undemanding, unconditional and non-judgemental nature of an animal beneficial because of their innate fear of both intimacy and criticism. They are likely to anthropomorphise their pet - the more human they can make them, the more they can have human-like undemanding interactions with them without all the complications and baffling emotions that ensue. An animal requires little in terms of emotional commitment and the pet, of course, will never leave the narcissist. If the narcissist treats the animal badly their survival instinct will cause it to 'forgive' the human.

It would appear that narcissists are, not surprisingly, drawn to extreme pets. One can imagine the overt narcissist swaggering with whichever dog has the most macho reputation at the time, the more showy and extreme the better. Of course that's not to say that everyone who owns an exotic or unusual animal is a narcissist just that someone with narcissistic tendencies may be drawn to the extremes in pet ownership, like many other areas in their lives. This trait in pet owning narcissists may be more subtle with a covert narcissist. They will often choose a pet that attracts attention in a different way, maybe with a teeny tiny pocket dog or an animal with a disability. Everyone will coo over the cutesy/injured animal and want to pet it. The narcissist can get their supply but still remain charmingly humble. They may complain quietly that this is really unwanted attention, they didn't ask for this and they can hardly walk two steps before people want to start a conversation. In reality, of course, this is a fountain of pure narcissistic supply.

Hal Herzog in an article on the Psychology Today[**] website[††] quotes from the findings of a recent study by Jennifer Vonk, a psychologist at Oakland University.

"People high in vulnerable (covert) narcissism were more attached to their pets—but only if the pet was unconventional."

†† https://www.psychologytoday.com/gb/blog/animals-and-us/201610/narcissism-and-exotic-pets-is-there-connection. Accessed 12 June 2018.

It would be an interesting research project to see if narcissistic behaviours, such as passive aggression and struggles for control are more prevalent in online groups that focus on extreme pets.

The narcissistic family

A family is a tyranny ruled by its weakest link

George Bernard Shaw

Realising that one or both parents are narcissistic may only become apparent when adult children are able to put words to the conduct that they have witnessed and eventually recognise that this is not normal family life.

For decades they may have accepted behaviours that have felt not quite right but have shrugged them off because 'that's our family.' They will accept the excuses made about the narcissist by their enablers who defend them with comments such as, 'That's just the way he is," "You're too sensitive". The child, whether ten or forty, is expected to ignore the unacceptable behaviour. After all, if they do find it unpalatable it is their own fault for being too delicate.

When the moment of realisation arrives, often decades later, it can be a shocking revelation, particularly if that child has since become an enabler. Suddenly the words and actions of narcissism can be unequivocally linked to the strange parenting behaviours experienced in their childhood. The adult child is now able to clearly see how they fit into the chaotic jigsaw puzzle of having a covert narcissist as one or both parents.

As children we tend to think that our family life is normal. Even if, as we get older, we experience family life that is different from our own we may still find that our default experiences are acceptable. As our own family may be based on the 'false self' of the narcissist, along with their enablers, and is all about public image we may at some unconscious level believe that all families work like this. The 'nice' family life that we experience with our friends we believe could be false because our own family can behave 'nicely' when they are on display to strangers. This may give us the warped illusion that all relationships, when on display to the public, are false.

At the time of writing, the Turpin family have been in the news. This is the story of the US couple who were arrested and charged with abuse and neglect which included allegedly chaining up and starving their thirteen children. Questions were asked as to why some of the adult children didn't escape and raise the alarm. Apparently they were sometimes taken on trips to Disneyland so may have had the opportunity. Maybe they felt that all families were structured in a similar way to their own. If they saw 'normal' families they probably assumed that this was just the 'public face' of that family, just as they were performing as a happy family in front of strangers.

In a less dramatic way this can be a similar scenario to that of a narcissistic family. If the family have a public face and a private face any psychological or emotional abuse may be seen as normal and universal by the children.

Children of narcissists may be isolated by their parents. They see their children as their possessions, rather than separate human beings that they bond with emotionally. They may have a tendency to control their lives more than is normal. Confusingly, the opposite can also occur. Self absorbed narcissistic parents can let their children run wild without parental supervision because they are too busy and distracted to parent in any conventional way.

Control might be demonstrated by a reluctance in letting their child have friends visit the house or allowing visits to other people's houses. At the root of this reluctance in allowing their children to socialise is that having their friends visiting involves the parent in some sort of 'task'. They might have to entertain the friends, but at the very least they have to put their public self on show. The narcissist can never be their natural selves in public, always the false self, so it can be exhausting if every casual visit involves them putting on the show. If they are doing it for their own 'friends' or relatives there is often an ulterior motive so the work is worth the effort. However, a child's friend is different. They still need to put on the public act because word might spread if they behave as badly as they would normally, yet they're not getting anything out of the situation. From this viewpoint it makes sense then to restrict the child from having visits from strangers. Their child visiting other people's houses is a little less stressful for the narcissist and at least gives them a break. All they have to worry about is if their child gives them away, so they don't want the child forming any close relationships with other families.

If the child returns with stories of the good time they had with their friend's family the narcissist will be horribly jealous. Narcissistic rage is likely to surface if the child returns and is too enthusiastic about how different the new family are to their own family. On hearing this the narcissist will either talk down the 'rival' family in some way and strongly discourage the child from becoming involved or will outright forbid the child from visiting for some obscure reason. As much as they don't connect to the child on an emotional level, they have their public image to consider. They have to appear to be the perfect parent and their child preferring another set of parents does not fit the story line.

A child of a narcissist parent is likely to be young when they realise the implications of admiring someone outside the family. It is possible that young children learn to 'grey rock' their narcissistic parents instinctively. Their sense of survival kicks in and they start to withhold information from their parents. They learn not to get hugely excited or disappointed because they know this will trigger a negative response in the parent. The parent might knock them down if they are excited about something and may even forbid them to go to an event or somehow sabotage it for them. If the child expresses disappointment, the parent may delight in their distress and tell them they deserve it or that it is totally their own fault.

There is little joy in the life of a child of a narcissist and they soon learn to keep a low profile, preferring to be on their own in their room rather than get involved in yet another argument that they can't win. They learn to keep their emotions passive and not antagonise or otherwise excite their parents. They may learn to double bluff and pretend that they're not desperately keen to go to an event because they know that the narcissistic parent will use their desperation as currency in one way or another, either to taunt them, or punish them for some 'crime'. They learn it is better to shrug their shoulders about what they want and hope they can sneak in a request when the parent is absorbed in their own world and not really paying attention. For the child it's like living with a sleeping dragon and they become skilled at the techniques needed to tip toe around it, trying not wake it up.

Love, or something that looks like love, is given but only conditionally by a narcissist. It's a reward not a right and as such it can be taken away. As the narcissist parent often sees their child as another possession they do not have the ability to attach at any deep level and any connection is superficial at best. However like other possessions such as a pet, they exist to show them in a good light and if they can gain reflected glory from a child's achievements then they will grab onto that with both hands.

However, in another narcissist twist although they want to make sure that they have a child they can be proud of in public they really don't want their child to outperform and outshine them. So they may sabotage the child if they see that they are beginning to do well. The narcissist will feel real pain if their child outperforms them and they need to keep them in their place i.e., in the family order that the narcissist has designated for them. They simply will not allow them to leapfrog the pecking order by virtue of their own merit. The sabotage may take the form of not allowing the child to go to university, purposely keeping them short of money and advising them against gaining all sorts of life enhancing skills. Oil will be thrown under their wheels at every opportunity to cause them to swerve. The narcissist parent is planning that by the time the child does eventually leave home they will have worn down their ambition so much that they will remain firmly below them in the place where they belong. They may want to keep them demoralised enough that even if they leave home they won't move too far away and they will still be dependent on the family enough to keep in close contact. Prepare for some ugly narcissistic rage if the victim spoils their plan by moving away with a partner, taking a job in another part of the country or moving abroad. They will use every trick in the book to prevent this from verbal abuse, laying on a guilt trip to feigning illness in order to get the victim to stay. A narcissist generally has huge abandonment issues and this kind of situation will push them to the edge. Many children of narcissists leave home at an early age, even if it means suffering the consequences of narcissistic rage. The relief felt at living on their own can be palpable after living all their lives under the pressure of constant censure and either close attention to their every move or disinterest.

By the time the children are adults they may have self esteem issues because they have never been allowed to think independently. On the surface, of course, the narcissist will deny this and insist that they have given their children every chance to develop and thrive. When the adult child finds a partner the narcissist parent might, at least initially put on their public persona for each family visit. The new partner might never see the narcissistic parent in full blown narcissistic mode. If the child has shared their experiences of growing up as a victim of narcissist abuse the new partner may express some doubt because as far as they are concerned the new mother or father in law is perfectly kind and charming and everything you could wish for in an in-law. This can be incredibly frustrating for the adult child as he tries to explain what they are 'really' like. The more they explain the more they seem, at best, bitter and twisted about insignificant experiences in their childhood and at worst a problematic liar. Either way they don't come out of this situation looking good. The narcissist is amused by how easy it is to fool the child's partner, but then they have been putting on this performance publicly for many years. The adult child may eventually think that their parent has changed or that maybe they imagined all that bad behaviour. Either way there is an uneasy, placid period in their relationship. Inevitably, however this can't last forever and there will be a slip. It might be an emergency or illness or any acute situation that causes the mask to slip, but slip it does. The new partner will be in shock as they see a full blown narcissistic tantrum for the first time and the adult child will feel all those familiar feelings of dread and fear, dredged up from childhood. At the same time they may feel relief that they have been vindicated and the new partner has finally seen through the veneer to the real person underneath. They're not going crazy, it was all true.

There is no recovery for the narcissist from this situation. After the emergency has passed they may revert to their old 'public' self but they are no longer fooling anyone and they know it. The mask will slip more often now. Make no mistake, walking into a narcissistic family is like walking into a bear pit.

There is another scenario that can play out with an adult child of narcissistic parents and this involves bringing a new romantic partner into the family who can immediately see straight through the complicated and delicate web of deceit that the narcissist has carefully nurtured over many years. It can be a major bombshell.

An outspoken partner of an adult child who is high on the emotional health spectrum and has no self esteem issues may just come out with something like 'Well this isn't normal, is it'? That can instantly break the spell. The curtains fall and the Emperor is revealed in his birthday suit! The narcissist panics and may present with full blown narcissistic rage as suddenly, everything they have built up appears to be under threat. In most scenarios it would seem that the narcissist will do what they can to rescue the situation and this is usually by quickly excluding the stranger. They will even go so far as to attempt to come between the couple and split them up. They will use every trick in the book in order to create problems for them including inventing stories about the new partner cheating. They may even encourage enablers to 'test' the new partner by inventing fake social media profiles and becoming a potential love interest. If the new partner either takes the bait or the narcissist can manipulate the situation to appear that they did they will triumphantly present their adult child with the 'evidence'. "Just leave him and come back home."

Or they may simply use guilt tactics on their adult child. "Look what this person is doing to our family. How can you let this happen?"

If their technique works the adult child will have learnt their lesson and next time will partner with someone who is less likely to say what they think in front of their parents. They may choose someone who is more compliant and less inclined to speak their mind. Alternatively they may school them before family get-togethers asking them to just ignore any weirdness. "They are strange, but it's just their way, we only have to stay for a couple of hours, please don't say anything."

If their plan to split the couple doesn't work the narcissist will exclude them by cutting off their own child in the process. They will have no compunction in doing this to stop the 'cancer' spreading amongst the family. They will not accept any dissension in the ranks. Of course they will spin this to make themselves look good, they will accept no blame, they are the victims and once again they can use their victim status to gain sympathy and narcissistic supply.

In some cases the narcissist will recruit allies to remove this cuckoo from the nest and will involve other adult children or extended members of the family. This will test family loyalties and when it comes to the rejection of the new partner and ultimately the discard of their adult child, it puts the rest of the family in the difficult position of having to choose a side. Invariably, the majority will stick with the narcissist. It's not rocket science that this will be the outcome because the person controlling the situation and calling the shots is a narcissist. It is their 'job' to be experts at manipulation and getting family members 'on side' was a plan from the beginning of the dispute.

At some point in the future the adult child may attempt to repair the relationship with their parent(s). The narcissist will fake compliance but when it comes to taking that first step there will be excuses. Often the narcissist will come up with another reason as to how their child has injured them and they will begin the whole cycle again.

To the world they are devastated that they have 'lost a child' but in reality they have no intention of ever letting that child back in their lives. If they do consider admitting the 'black sheep' back into the fold they will only do so under certain circumstances, the most important one being that they are no longer with the outsider who, in their eyes, has caused so much destruction to the family. There will be terms and conditions for returning to the family because, after all, for the narcissist, all love is conditional and rules must be obeyed before you can be forgiven.

It's interesting, with a view to narcissist parents, to search google for terms like 'my son's girlfriend is stealing him away from me'. This search term provides many links to 'agony aunt' columns where 'adult child theft' appears to be a relatively common scenario. Advice generally from other readers, seems to be that it's not surprising that the son doesn't want to be around such a controlling, bitter and jealous mother and you should be glad that he's found happiness. Of course the narcissist will have a much stronger justification for not liking the new partner. They will be able to quote chapter and verse about how controlling and evil the new boyfriend or girlfriend is, but in reality it is all about a loss of control for themselves and possibly a new family dynamic where the facade of the perfect family is transparent to the stranger.

This period in a narcissistic family is a particularly dangerous time with potential flash points for conflict. In an emotionally healthy family it can be difficult when young adults are finding their feet, testing relationships with raging hormones and all that entails. However for a narcissist parent it is fraught with difficulties when new and 'untrained' people enter their bubble and are not afraid to say what they see.

Unconditional love

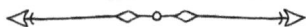

Unconditional love is a concept that is difficult for a narcissist to grasp, although, on one level, they use the term freely themselves to point out flaws in other people, for some reason it doesn't apply to them and their actions. Incidentally and perversely the narcissist is often the same person who fills their social media page with family quotes and protestations about how family is everything. A case of 'the narcissist doth protest too much, methinks'. We have to remind ourselves that this is their public image not their feelings.

When we hear about a serial killer still being visited in prison by his mother, we're not surprised because we accept that some bonds are so strong that it doesn't matter what crime he has committed, she is still his mother. We might feel repulsed by the criminal and the crime, but nevertheless we are able to understand the bond and the unconditional love that exists between a child and parent. A narcissist, on the other hand, may cut off a child because, for example, they have a different political opinion. The narcissist will go to great lengths to justify this action and will have no qualms in publicly humiliating their child to prove their point, even going so far as to use social media to berate and disown them. I have heard of cases where a parent will even publicly state that they have only one child, when in reality they have two. One who agrees with everything they say and one who doesn't.

One clue you may be dealing with a narcissist is when a parent or family member starts a sentence with "I love you, but.. (insert the victims faults here). This is indicative of complete misunderstanding of the term unconditional love. Conditions are being attached to this love. There are rules to their 'love'. You don't 'deserve' their love if you don't meet their conditions or expectations. If you don't obey their rules which might be, leave your husband because we don't like him. Or how dare you leave home and abandon me. There are no compromises, no negotiations it's my way or the highway, quite literally.

The narcissist prides themselves on being the calm

and rational member of the family which is no surprise. It's easy to be dispassionate and apparently rational when you have no genuine feelings for other people.

SOCIAL MEDIA

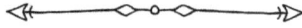

Intro

Social networking sites (SNS) and the narcissist are an area of interest that is likely to become a significant petri dish for behavioural scientists in the future. As of now, we're only just beginning to understand the insidious nature of the malignant covert narcissist and just how much damage and chaos they can cause when they spread their particular type of malice online.

The manipulation of multiple victims and the struggle for what they perceive as power is being played out, in public, in front of our eyes. Cyber-bullying, mobbing, gaslighting, baiting and other tactics employed by the narcissist can contribute to the distress and, in some cases, ongoing mental health problems for their victims.

We may be aware of attempts to manipulate in 'real life' because we may, even unconsciously, recognise warning signs. Body language and tone of voice can alert us to words that don't match actions and that something is not quite right. If we are lucky or perceptive we may have a 'gut feeling' about some people. Online interactions have none of these signals and we may be unaware that we are being subjected to carefully prepared social media posts that are designed to engender a particular response.

However, knowledge offers us protection and if we can recognise warning signs when narcissists are using social media, we can not only avoid problematic people ourselves but also spread the word to a wider audience.

Many narcissists use social media primarily because platforms such as Facebook, Twitter and Instagram provide an abundance of narcissistic supply. It's important to remember that narcissists are always seeking attention and are insatiable in their desire to create a coterie of adoring fans. They need constant validation from external sources and social media is the ideal medium to provide this stimuli. At any time of day or night, if an ego needs stroking, Facebook or Instagram is available with the ability to generate a kind word or compliment from one of thousands of 'friends'.

Narcissists tend to have a lot of online friends because they actively encourage quantity over quality given their preference for shallow and weak relationships. They will accept any friend request and sometimes even use one of the apps that are available to buy 'friends' and 'likes' in bulk. They see the number of friends they can acquire as a trophy. The higher the number the more important they are and this self delusion occurs, incredibly, even when they've paid for 'friends'. Thus they are perfectly suited to an online environment with fleeting and tenuous relationships.

However, one of the myths perpetrated by the mainstream media and their simplistic interpretation of narcissism is the idea that the narcissist is constantly pulling out their phone to communicate with their friends. This is not usually the case because narcissists do not crave social interaction, only attention and adoration. They may be checking how many 'likes' their latest post has received, but they really don't want to interact with the people who are following them. They tend to write about themselves but rarely comment on other people's posts because frankly, what other people think or say about their own lives is not really of any interest to them. The main focus for the narcissist on social media is to get positive feedback about their activities. This tends to result in a constant churn of friends as some people tire of the one way relationship.

The narcissist is happiest with 'friends' and followers who are strangers to them, preferably living across the other side of the world. They can pick them up and drop them with ease and there is never any messy 'real' confrontations. They will quickly ditch anyone who wants genuine interaction and becomes too demanding, they really don't want to waste their time on idle chit chat. In a group situation the narcissist will filter members so the group develops into a concentrated following of admirers who are undemanding and only serve to provide narcissistic supply.

Narcissists will gravitate towards celebrities to endorse them and expand their online reach. They may want a famous person to retweet their latest venture in order to give it authenticity and/or enhance their business and they will often appeal to base emotions to achieve this end. Their latest project may include elements based on the cute or tear-jerking and be sycophantic in the extreme to gain the attention of their chosen celebrity. Sometimes these moves can look accidental, casual and completely unplanned. But with a narcissist these will be organised like a military campaign.

However, they often struggle when they step outside their own pool of admirers. They will be truly puzzled that a celebrity doesn't respond to their heartfelt or witty tweets or Facebook posts. Maybe they didn't see them. They can't believe that someone could read their brilliance and not respond. If the celebrity continues to ignore their increasingly desperate cries for attention the narcissist will discard that celebrity, who will then change from an object of admiration to a hated target who the narcissist will happily badmouth to anyone willing to listen. If, against all odds, they do manage to catch the eye of a celebrity the narcissist will name-drop shamelessly and imply a relationship that is much closer than it is in reality.

The outgoing overt and the quiet covert narcissist will use social media in completely different ways. The overt will unashamedly brag about their lifestyle, their car, their house and their appearance, constantly posting selfies and informing the world about how great they are. They rarely engage with their 'friends'. On Twitter, for example, they will be the one who acts like a celebrity by never following anyone back. They may have 4,000 followers and only follow 10 people themselves. They don't want their feed cluttered up with riff-raff. Why would they want to read all the rubbish that these inferior people post? It's not difficult to spot an overt narcissist using social media.

A covert, as you might guess, is a little more difficult to identify. They have the same tendency to not comment on posts that don't involve them in some way, but their posts are not as openly bragging. They are masters of the humble brag, self deprecating to an extent that will garner comments from friends that reinforce their feelings of self worth. "You are a wonderful person, please don't put yourself down" followed by another hundred affirmations. They are much more subtle in their interactions, putting time aside to share worthy posts about charitable events or missing pets. They will also shamelessly over sentimentalise in order to manipulate their audience.

Social media is often used by the narcissist to enhance their reputation and as a platform to recruit and train their flying monkeys or enablers. They are able to use their manipulative skills to increase their 'fan' base and then manipulate them in a way that would make a reality talent show producer proud.

It's important to remember when using social media that the narcissist, although disadvantaged in many areas of life, is highly skilled in others. I'm going to assume that you are not an expert at manipulating people and that you haven't spent your whole life honing your skills in order to always get your own way . The narcissist has, and they will alter their social media posts in the middle of the night, use Photoshop to change wording on documents, use fake accounts to accuse you of extraordinary 'crimes' and threaten exposure, even litigation, if you retaliate. All the while being the benign, lovable, charitable, talented, witty and clever person to their group of enablers. They are the experts at this and they will never let you win, not at any cost.

They will be making up the most outrageous lies and totally fictitious imaginings about you. One of the disadvantages they may have is that they have removed themselves so far from your life that they really don't know you at all, other than what they can glean from your social media presence, so instead they will fictionalise your life. Members of their group, who have never even met you, might join in and before you know it you have been turned into a bizarre and fabricated version of yourself.

Our default is trust

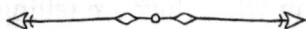

O f course, many aspects of social media are beneficial, but it can also be a minefield pockmarked with narcissists who are difficult to identify at first glance.

One of the red flags that may signal a problem is if a friend or family dispute is published in a public environment, such as Facebook, particularly if you discover that the other party has been banned, blocked or otherwise shut down. Inviting several hundred people, many of whom you don't actually know outside of Facebook, to comment and involve themselves in a family dispute is probably not the most helpful way to resolve an issue. Of course, many are likely to support the accuser because they are 'friends' and they are only seeing the evidence and hearing the complaints from one side.

It must be inbuilt into humans to trust what we read. Newspapers are a good example. We know that they are not always truthful. If you've ever been the subject of a newspaper report no matter how innocuous inevitably there will be mistakes ranging from spelling your name wrong to something more serious, maybe misrepresenting your opinion. Yet when we read newspapers, whether online or in print our first instinct is to believe what we read, maybe even sharing that information with others without thinking. Our first instinct is not to check sources and research the story, we tend to trust the information until it's proven to be inaccurate. Our default is trust.

Similarly, with social media, we tend to trust what we read unless we are presented with evidence that it isn't true. We tend to believe that the person who is presenting as the kindly, charitable, kid and animal loving person is just that, based on not much more than what they are telling us. Intellectually if we're asked if we believe everything we're told, of course we'll say no, because we're discerning, right? But in the cosy confines of our social media pages if someone tells us they're a duck we'll believe them, until the crocodile emerges from the water and sinks its teeth into our arm.

For a narcissist this is a rich area for exploitation and they may work on many levels. The obvious one is romantically. Getting to know a potential partner online before you meet them gives opportunities to prime the innocent with lies, to set up a completely different persona and love bomb. The reality may be something different, but luring an innocent into the narcissist's trap is easier with social media.

The downside of social media for a narcissist is that it's difficult to play one of their ace cards - gaslighting. The ability to save screenshots and posts that have been uploaded is a distinct disadvantage to a narcissist. It's difficult to protest that they didn't say something when it is possible to produce proof of exactly what they did say. However, every now and then, they will become so comfortable on social media in the kingdom they have created for themselves they may let their guard down. If someone challenges them on anything, and I do mean anything at all, they let fly with a tirade that seems completely out of character to their followers. In fact the narcissist may immediately delete the offending article or tweet and offer the explanation that they have been hacked. This serves the double purpose of distracting the group from their rant and engendering sympathy. They have to provide an explanation that will keep their audience 'on side'. If saying that their account has been hacked isn't appropriate or believable then the back story will be provided. By this I mean a long post about how they've been wronged for a long time but have never spoken publicly about it, because that's not the kind of person they are. But now, the person that has been persecuting them has worn them down and they just snapped. They are sorry about losing control and really sorry that their friends had to witness it. And there you have a negative turned into a positive for our narcissist. Not only have they negated their outburst, they have formed a stronger bond with their group by apparently exposing their own vulnerability and demonstrating their human weakness.

They have also begun the demonisation of their victim in the most effective way possible. It leaves the way open to begin a public smear campaign championed by dozens or maybe hundreds of people who have no idea what is really going on and innocently cheer on the narcissist in their fight for 'justice' Additionally, when they feel that the adoration within their group is waning they can relight interest by dropping in a sympathy inducing incident about how they have been, once again, the victim of this awful person. Once more this will result in the unsuspecting rallying their support and being even more vehement in their hatred of the person perpetrating this horrible vendetta against their 'leader'.

If the narcissist feels that they need further proof of being victimised, they may step it up a gear and manufacturer 'evidence'. He or she may create a bogus profile on a social network site and post outrageous abuse directed towards themselves. They will take a screenshot, post it to their supporters and say something along the lines of… "I'm so sorry that I (insert bad behaviour here) but life has been extremely stressful lately and this is the sort of abuse I have to put up with." And there you have it. Immediate distraction from their own bad behaviour, a ton of sympathetic and supportive posts, and maybe even some retribution for the perpetrator of this terrible deed. All without getting their hands dirty. Of course, the narcissist will not accuse their victim directly of publishing this scandalously abusive post, but the implication will be obvious. The group will have been primed to expect any negative behaviour towards their 'leader' to be initiated by the usual suspect, who is, in reality the narcissist's victim. The response from his group will satisfy the narcissist's hunger for supply, for a while.

The more perceptive members of the group may recognise this dubious manipulative behaviour and slip away. They are smart enough to realise that calling out this conniving conduct and initiating a confrontation with this type of person is rarely productive and instead they quietly leave the group. Alternatively if they don't want the narcissist to realise that they've left they may just mute them. This natural filtering concentrates the group into those who are left being the most fervent supporters and/or the most gullible.

Group manipulation

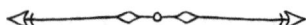

O bserving the manipulation of groups on social media is as fascinating as it is disturbing. Narcissists are the crack addicts of the attention seeking world and the temptation to belong to an online group of undemanding people who adore them is almost impossible to resist.. Once established and comfortable within a group they may then attempt to take it over. After all they are so knowledgeable and everyone else is stupid in comparison, they would be able to do a much better job. After an initial period of being charming and engaging members with their caring, clever and witty persona, they will first offer to help out, maybe with admin and then they will quietly begin the take over process. They really need to have ultimate control and they don't wish to bow to anyone else's authority.

In large groups, there may be a number of narcissists and a weaker, less established narcissist may recognise a more powerful narcissist and will not usually engage them in a direct confrontation. If they feel that the group leader will not let their power go easily they will use alternative techniques. This may involve becoming the victim of a more powerful member. They will manufacture a dispute and instead of displaying anger at this 'victimisation' they become sad, vulnerable and apologetic for everything that has happened. Using this ploy they will gradually get a proportion of the membership to believe that they are truly a victim. Once they have signalled their discontent about their 'bully' to enough people they may start their own group. It will be similar to the original group but with some obvious differences. Typically it will not have any of the rules of the old group.

The narcissist will invite their new found allies to join the break away group. They don't want to cause any trouble, of course, oh no, perish the thought! However. they feel a new group would be a positive move forward because, on a personal level, they would be able to escape the 'bullying' which is causing them, and more importantly, their family such stress. Do not doubt for a moment that they will use their family at every opportunity - it's not that they are weak themselves, of course, they are just protecting their family.

The second reason for starting up on their own is that they feel a new group would be different because it would address - insert any kind of justification here. Using this method they will succeed in stealing enough members to make their group viable and to work up to the next stage.

In the early days of the new group they will put in a lot of effort to maintain and grow the membership. They will respond to comments and questions in super quick time. They will be kind and courteous. They will offer to publicise any good cause. They will emphasise the fact that this group doesn't need silly rules. Just be kind. If the group is about a particular specialist subject they will research it intensely and generously share their research with group members. The group will become an informative, funny, safe space.

The motivation for growing this membership differs from narcissist to narcissist. At least initially it may be purely for narcissistic supply. As the 'boss' of the group they will be offered respect and even hero worship by some members. This is catnip to a narcissist. Over time however, if the group is successful they may look at ways to monetise the people who hang on every word and this may become the main motivation to continue.

Whatever the motivation is for continuing, if the narcissist gets bored, needs more supply or feels under threat, they may use the common technique of hinting about the possibility of closing down the group and leaving forever. Of course it's not only narcissists that do this but it is a technique favoured by narcissists as a manipulation tool to pull their group together. We can presume that the narcissist is providing something to the group, maybe funny, 'feel good', sentimental, 'authentic' posts that are used to prime this particular audience and keep them coming back for more. The members have come to rely on their leader as a necessary part of their day.

If someone publicly disagrees with the leader or challenges their authority the statements of 'I can't do this any more, I'm leaving', are not automatically flagged up as a sign of manipulation. Empathetic group members will feel that this is a wonderful person at the end of their tether. They need to support them and encourage them to stay. 'Please don't go', 'Don't let them win!'. This supportive response from their group is like manna from heaven, feeding their need for supply. A good indication of knowing if this is real is that the narcissist will rarely actually leave. That was never the intention, they only wanted their group to beg them to stay. It is likely that they don't even take a break. After a period of tension-building indecision, the climax of the show is that they are finally persuaded to stay and are then likely to write a long post apologising for the interruption to their normal, happy and fun posts. They don't know what came over them to be dragged down by this one particular person and they can't thank the group enough for their support. They will gush and the emotional post that accompanies the resumption of normal service will make people cry!

The group will feel good, they had a moment of panic imagining that someone who has become a part of their lives might just disappear forever. Now, not only have they persuaded them to stay they have also offered support. They will feel even more committed.

In addition to the relief that their leader is not leaving group members may also experience anger. They may be angry towards the person who purportedly caused the drama and has pushed their 'friend' to this extreme point, threatening the existence of the group itself. If it happens again their hero might really leave and this 'family' will be destroyed. Vilification of the person who upset the narcissist is now much more likely to be accepted as deserved. Even death threats may be acknowledged as justified. It's reasonable to assume that the people that are tacitly accepting of these threats are non-violent, law abiding people who in real life would be appalled if a friend suggested that murder would be a genuine solution to a problem relationship. However, in this particular social media situation they have been groomed, and I use that word carefully, to accept this is as normality.

If someone ventures to raise their head above the parapet and dares to question the narcissist about a threat of violence, then of course, it was just a joke and the questioner is being a bit too sensitive. Maybe they will be labelled a 'snowflake'. If the questioner persists, this is likely to unleash narcissistic rage. At the very least, that person will be banned from the group and likely blocked from making any contact with the narcissist ever again. The narcissist will see this a threat to their public image and they are likely to react in an inappropriately forceful way.

The narcissist as a group leader performs a delicate juggling act, because they will want to appear to encourage openness and honesty, and yet if any insubordination is directed at them in the way of questioning their words or actions then swift retaliation will follow. If they have to ban a member there is likely to be a long and public explanation. They will not want to ignore the ban because of their para- noia that people will be talking about them, or worse, maybe plotting behind their back. So they will write long posts that justify their actions, 'in the spirit of openness', and analyse what motivated this person to question them. They are likely to hint at a conspiracy, that they are in cahoots with their enemy, you know the person we think it's probably a good idea to murder.

This post will soothe the narcissist because they will get validation from other members who have been primed to agree with anything they say. It will also serve as a warning to other group members. Do anything to cross the leader and retaliation will be swift and brutal. You will be shunned.

Once we become aware of the strategies employed by people who are high on the narcissistic spectrum it is disturbing to see how easily people in groups can be manipulated. In forms of popular culture, for example, reality television in the form of talent shows, we may be much more aware of the techniques used to pull at our emotions, yet we are still prepared to subject ourselves to the manipulation in exchange for the reward of entertainment. In a group dynamic it can be more difficult to see what is going on, because our default setting is not to be cynical about the people who we believe to be our friend. We're not looking for the equivalent of the swelling music in every interaction.

In a real life situation, we may be wary of problematic people by their use of micro expressions and body language. Unconsciously, we may feel something is 'off' and instinctively pull away from the relationship. With the online narcissist it is more difficult. The narcissist does not naturally have feelings of empathy and compassion, and they have had to pay careful attention to others in order to replicate emotions in their everyday life. Their whole life has been based on this study to evaluate what works and what doesn't and that, in turn, makes them efficient liars. They lie about everyday events that they have no need to lie about. "Why would they even lie about that?" an incredulous co-worker or family member might say, but they are constantly practising and honing this 'skill', so that when they need it for something more important they have all the nuances and body language needed to succeed in their subterfuge. For a narcissist then, lying is part of their everyday routine, so lying on social media is child's play. With online lying there is no body language or micro expressions to worry about, no slip of the tongue. They can hone and polish their words carefully before posting and we, as normal human beings with our default setting of trust will not suspect that we are being played.

Of course if this scenario were to appear on day one of our relationship with a narcissist we might consider that there are two sides to every story, but the narcissist will have that covered. In their group they have thoroughly established their 'good person' persona. When a member balances this against the rantings, ravings, bad language and generally out of control crazy person that appears to be waging a war on our hero, the outcome is a done deal.

If a new person joins the group social proof will, for the most part, determine how they form a judgement about the situation, ie they will assume that established members who know the full story have more knowledge about the dispute and they will fall in with the crowd. It's sobering to consider how easily led we are. At our core, we are pack animals and if someone looks at the sky we all look at the sky. The narcissist finds it easy to manipulate a crowd, particularly online. They will get pleasure from how superior they feel when pulling the strings of these enablers. Again, I would emphasise that many of these people are completely innocent. Although one can't excuse the more extreme actions of this group, the motivation has been orchestrated by the untruthful narcissist.

Once a narcissist feels confident in the love and praise from their own group, which appears to be unconditional, they may venture out into the wider world of the internet.

The story here may be quite different.

For example, in their own group they may be seen as a teller of the funniest jokes, they may get many 'likes' and virtual applause, when they tell a joke to their own audience. The group members may not actually think the jokes are that funny, but they enjoy other aspects of the group so they hit the like button. The comedian becomes confident in their ability to be hilarious and they venture outside their group to a comedy website where people can try out their jokes. They bomb. The people there are not shy to offer constructive criticism about why the would-be comedian is not funny and how he or she could improve, but our narcissist is not interested in hearing any criticism, no matter how constructive. They are really only interested in the adoration and not in improving their comedy routine, so they quickly scuttle back to their own group, tell a few jokes and, phew... the love is still there.

One of the narcissist's biggest fears and threat to their public persona is criticism. The slightest criticism will send them into paroxysms of rage. In order to avoid that situation the covert narcissist will privately recognise their limitations. In their own group, however, they still position themselves as the expert in their field. If they are encouraged by members of their group to go further and try for world domination, the covert, who has already tested the waters and not found them welcoming will be ready with plausible excuses. Better to have the adoration of their group, groomed as they have been to populate the narcissist's fantasy world than venture into the choppy waters of reality.

The Untouchables

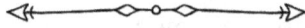

W e are generally not so gullible that we can't see through some of the more obvious manipulation techniques used on social media and we may mock the obvious hard sells, the cheesy posts extolling us to better ourselves by buying a self help course, etc. However, the savvy covert narcissist will focus in on an area that will be free from criticism. They may be self aware enough to realise that they are likely to lose control and risk exposing their real persona if they are publicly criticised, so including an element in their project that cannot be criticised is a given. We have seen how some of the worst abusers in recent times have attached themselves to charitable work as a shield. Nobody can publicly criticise a person who generously gives their time and money to charity, can they?

There are several areas of interest that have potential for a covert narcissist including children, animals and the military. The narcissist is aware that by focussing on one of these they can call on a large section of the population to support them without question. Without question. It really is worth repeating. The narcissist will already have scored points for being involved in this area, "They must be a good guy if they work with kids/cats/veterans, right?" and if they can find a product, sentimentalise it and every now and again make people shed a tear over it, they are onto a winner. This may seem cynical and it is.

The narcissist can expertly judge a mood and exploit it for their own ends and will be able to turn tragedies into successes for themselves. For example, if their cat dies they will write heart rending posts in their group and possibly have to take time off work because they are so devastated. This is not so unusual,we are, of course, attached to our pets. However, people who are close to the narcissist may be surprised at the emotional outpouring because they didn't think they even liked the cat. They were forever complaining about it, ignoring and borderline neglecting it and they had seen them kick it on more than one occasion. Here though, the narcissist has grabbed an opportunity to gain narcissistic supply by using a method that nobody can question. If anyone did challenge them on the genuineness of their emotions they and everyone in their group would be outraged.

The narcissist has no real feelings behind this, they have just learnt that people will like them/buy their product if they display this sort of emotion for their chosen subject and are able to generate these emotions in others. They have trained their whole lives to manipulate and they are good at it. Moreover, they know that they can't be openly criticised if they choose an 'untouchable' subject. Who would dare to speak out against someone who is carrying out charitable work and supports such a worthy organisation. In reality, the narcissist's involvement with the charity will be superficial at best. They might share the charity's fund raising posts in their group and urge others to support them, but in terms of practical support there will be little, if any at all.

Revenge

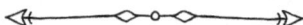

A narcissist is the ultimate grudge keeper. They will remember any slight, real or imagined and extract revenge in any way they can, sometimes years later. If you are not behaving as they want, you have disobeyed their commands, or have in any way exposed them they will be relentless in finding ways to make you suffer. If they find they can't control you they will almost certainly initiate a smear campaign. This is likely to involve exposing or threatening to expose private information they have been holding about you, waiting for the perfect moment to expose it.

Another trick they use is to ask questions that may sound innocent but are designed to cause trouble. For example a narcissist might be conducting a vendetta against an ex-friend who has posted a photo taken in a shopping mall, on their Facebook page. The narcissist might contact the company that owns the shopping mall to enquire if anyone is allowed to take photos on their private property. When the reply comes that it is possible but only with permission, the narcissist will say that they just wanted to check because they'd seen a photo..and they'll forward a link to the company, safe in the knowledge that their ex-friend will not have asked permission and relishing any trouble that this might cause.

Virtue signalling

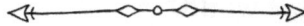

irtue signalling is a phrase that has leapt into common usage over the last five years. The wiki definition is

'the conspicuous expression of moral values primarily with the intent of enhancing standing within a social group.' The term was first used in signalling theory, to describe any behaviour that could be used to signal virtue, especially piety among the religious'.

It is often used as a criticism by one political group against another who they feel is trying to take the moral high ground to instigate public concern or outrage. In a more generalised and localised way it is also used, particularly on social media platforms, to describe the act of posting articles and links that demonstrate what caring and charitable people we are. We may have seen this happening ourselves, the friend who constantly posts photos that make us feel that the world is an awful place, pictures of animals being horribly abused, an elderly person has been mugged and they make the obvious comments, for example - this must stop NOW! Apparently the rest of us think it's perfectly okay to do this and we need to be told, usually in CAPITAL LETTERS that it's unacceptable. They don't actually do anything about it, the post doesn't come with a 'call to action', to go on a march or volunteer at a community project. The sole purpose of the post is to point back at themselves and signal to everyone what a caring individual they are to make us aware of these atrocities. It's an easy way of manufacturing a persona. If we are presented with this view of them often enough we will indeed start to believe that this is a truly caring person, alerting us to what needs changing in the world.

Public versus private posts

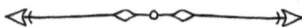

Another tactic to look out for are comments or posts that have the sole intention of talking to a wider audience rather than the person they are purportedly talking to. This is a dead giveaway. So, for example, an adult daughter might be having a conversation, in a public post on Facebook with her mother who lives in the next street. Mother might mention that she's had a hard day and the daughter will comment, "Not to worry, I'll come round later and I'll take you out in my shiny new sports car. I know that always cheers you up."

Obviously her mother knows about the car so the inclusion of "shiny new sports car" is not a message to her but to inform a wider audience. This type of clumsy attempt to induce jealousy in her enemies is more common than we might imagine and is easy to spot.

At the time of writing (2018) most social media platforms allow a degree of privacy when its members post photographs. For example on Facebook there are various privacy options for photos from only you can see to making it available for the whole world, with various degrees in between.

When a narcissist discards a friend or family member they will often ban and block them on Facebook so the shunned member can't see or respond to any of their posts.

In their mind this makes sense, they have cut off this person and they do not want any interaction with them on their social media page in case they are exposed. The victim might dispute what they are saying, they might tell the truth. In the interests of their public image they need to silence them.

It's interesting then when we see that the narcissist will occasionally post a photo that is set to public i.e., the whole world can see it. A mistake? No, the narcissist takes social media manipulation extremely seriously and rarely makes a genuine mistake. The photo will invariably be a carefully constructed happy family photo which will appear to everyone as perfectly innocent. However, one has to ask the question, why, when they are always so careful about posting only to friends has this been posted for everyone to see? The answer invariably is that although it looks like an innocent family photo it really is a weapon for the narcissist who is anticipating that their victim will make a fake profile in order to view their public posts. This, of course, is one of the narcissist's own trademarks. They have numerous fake profiles in order to 'collect evidence' to use against their victim. Their plan, with the public posting of a photos, is that the carefully manufactured image will make their victim feel excluded and unhappy because they would once have been in that photo. They used to belong to that 'beautiful family'.

So here's the thing, if you have a friend or family member and they complain about the responses to their innocent picture, take a look at their posts. If their usual practice is to post photos that are available to 'friends only' but this particular post is 'public', then it's a safe bet that this one is purely for taunting in order to elicit an angry response. You may not realise how the narcissist is silently goading their target, but the target will. If the plan works and they get an angry response, the narcissist can then play the role of victim in front of their friends and get their much needed narcissist supply, at the same time the real victim is re-victimised.

You may be thinking that this degree of planning and manoeuvring must be an exaggeration. Who would spend this amount of time and energy on setting up a victim on Facebook. The answer, of course is a narcissist. Their public image is their lifeblood and social media platforms are the ideal playground for their manipulative games. We, in our innocence, take what they are saying at face value. After all who has time to be a detective and look deeper into their posts. They rely on this and, of course, will feign complete innocence if they are challenged. It's a sobering thought that it is estimated that one in ten people fall into the cluster B personality type category. If you think of that in terms of the people on a social media platform like Facebook then it's not out of this world to think that at least one or two of our friends are involved in this kind of manipulation and subterfuge and we may be blissfully unaware. Personally, I know that after carrying out this research for several years it does make me think twice when someone starts complaining about being victimised. Two sides to every story has never been so relevant.

Cultural snobbery

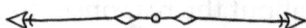

A nother technique that a narcissist may employ when using social networking sites is mockery. A cerebral narcissist is constantly looking for ways to flaunt their superior intellect and mocking popular culture is an effective vehicle. In this case the narcissist may use disparagement disguised as humour in an attempt to malign or belittle an individual victim or a group who they feel is inferior.

We all have different tastes and we pick and choose, for example, what we watch on television according to those tastes. If we enjoy a particular show, we may post about it to our friends on social media in order to share that experience with others. If we find that we really dislike a show, or worse, we judge something without watching it at all, fewer of us will post our opinion online. We don't want to potentially offend our friends who may love the show and we certainly don't want to start an online battle over a TV show. It's a matter of judgement and everyone has a different opinion. Mine is no more important than yours.

However for the cerebral narcissist the temptation to flaunt their superior intellect and taste is greater than the risk of upsetting people. They will gleefully mock popular culture often using humour as a vehicle. If they are ever confronted they can use the, now familiar, defence of, "it was just a joke". So if you're a fan of Breaking Bad or Game of Thrones your narcissist may repost hating memes on social media and will complain that they just don't get the appeal and probably give a little shudder, thus reinforcing their superior intellect and your inferiority.

The narcissist is also likely to be fond of obscure music whether that might be in the form of a less popular bands from the 80s or local musicians who haven't yet found fame. The more obscure the better to display their superior cultural tastes on social networking sites. You may also notice that they make comments like, "I used to like Adele back in the day, before she was discovered but not now." They really don't want to be lumped in with the 'common people'. Cultural snobbery for the cerebral narcissist is pretty much a given.

Yet another form of mockery favoured by the covert narcissist is as the spelling or grammar police of the internet. If someone has posted a reasoned and thoughtful post on Facebook but there is a spelling mistake the narcissist will pounce on it, ignore the reasoned argument and instead mock the error. This makes them feel superior in a way that is 'helping to educate the world' one spelling mistake at a time. The real purpose of course is to humiliate and embarrass the writer of the post. It's a relatively acceptable form of mockery in an environment that knows nothing about the writer who may be struggling with dyslexia or another disability. Even with this lack of knowledge the narcissist will not be able to resist parading their superior education and intellect.

Projection also plays a part in this kind of mockery. A narcissist will often taunt their victim about a topic which they themselves are highly sensitive about. If they have always been the shortest person in their circle of friends and they have reason to engage in hostilities with someone who happens to be shorter, guess which will be the first insult thrown? Likewise with spelling and grammar. The previous holder of 'most likely to make spelling mistakes in the group' will make social media posts mocking the spelling of a new member, sometimes even complete with spelling mistakes, seemingly unaware of the irony.

This projection serves the double purpose of making themselves feel better because they are now not the 'worst' and also inhibits the victim from using the same topic to retaliate. Few people resort to the 'You're just as bad' argument for fear of descending into a tit-for-tat, nursery playground argument.

Goading

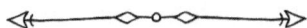

Goading is a sport to the narcissist. If they have been through the idealisation, devalue and discard cycle they will often use goading to throw out challenges to their victim. The narcissistic rage that caused the shunning will never leave them and even if they have no contact with their victim they still want to keep them close. Getting them to react to a goading post on a social networking site is about point scoring. Every interaction is a bonus.

In order to protect their public persona they will carefully start to drip feed to their enablers, in a slow and calculated way, details of their victim and their craziness. They feel so sorry for this poor deluded person, they obviously have mental health issues and although they've tried hard to help them it's now got to the point that they need to get on with their own lives, because they can't take the abuse any longer. It's beginning to affect their own health.

They will soften their audience, and at this point they will be getting at least a handful of support posts, ie "How terrible for you", "I'm so sorry you're having to go through this." "You are such a lovely person to have to suffer this." etc etc. To consolidate this they then need a concrete example of their victim's crazy behaviour, so they will time a post for when they will be almost certain that their victim will be active on that particular platform. They may now post an openly abusive message, but make it look like they are responding to something the victim has said. Ideally it will contain a piece of gaslighting that is so untrue that the victim will be provoked into making a confused and angry response.

If the narcissist gets a response to the abusive post, they may immediately delete their own 'bait' post, hoping that most of their followers will never have seen it. They can then point to their victim's 'unprovoked and abusive' post as an example of mental instability and bathe in the unbridled sympathy and support that comes from their group. There is a risk that someone may have seen their original post, but if they are ever called on it they will explain it as a minor aber-ration, they have been pushed to the limit, they should never have posted it, they regretted it immediately, it's not how they would normally respond and that's why they deleted it. They are ashamed of it. Of course this 'confession' of weakness will generate even more responses of support from the majority of their group of followers. The other method a narcissist who is concerned about their public image will use to disguise toxic posts, is to post their abuse as a comment on a friend's account. They have no qualms about using a friend, ideally a friend who doesn't have many mutual friend's in common, to start a war of words. They can play as dirty as they like on somebody else's page because none of their own group will see the tirade.

After a few weeks have gone by, they will even feel confident in denying that they have EVER posted anything on social media that could be upsetting to the their victim. This naturally infuriates the victim and they may start to take screenshots of abusive posts and publish them. This has the effect of stopping, to some extent the narcissist from posting abuse instead resorting to the dog whistle type of attack.

Of course the victim does not have access to the narcissist's group, they will have been banned or blocked much earlier, in fact the moment that they said anything that disagreed with the narcissist in public. This is the key word, public. The narcissist is so emotionally empty that their whole life is centred around obtaining validation and praise from strangers, and any threat to that public persona is, for them, threatening their very existence.

At this point the victim feels frustrated, angry and persecuted. They have no way of rebutting these claims being made about them publicly and the constant baiting may, in fact, bring about the damage to their mental health that the narcissist has been so busy telling anyone who will listen. The narcissist's fake concern can be nauseating to those who know the real story.

There is another side to goading and that involves the narcissist who becomes so comfortable in their own group to the extent that anything they do to their victim is 'fair game'. In other words they are able to openly publish abusive and provocative posts aimed at their victim and their group have become so indoctrinated that there is no need for the narcissist to hide their glee when the victim responds with upset and anger. They may make comments that openly display their pride that the baiting has worked such as 'oops I think I may have upset someone' or boast about their successful 'fishing trip'. This post will garner many likes because in the eyes of the group any action is now justified.

As an objective outsider it can be fascinating to watch a narcissist who becomes confident in the unwavering support of their group. As we unravel the dog whistles and goading, the more we are able to see dysfunction exposed.

Empathy mocking and attachment

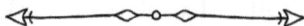

I f we pay attention, we can observe how the narcissist exposes themselves, particularly on social networking sites, by mocking empathy and boasting about their lack of attachment. They see empathy as weak behaviour but conversely they also see how it is valued by society. Although their fake self is usually on display complete with fabricated emotions and socially appropriate comments, just occasionally, particularly when they are angry, their true feelings will bubble up and they will openly mock the empathy of others. They may use the term 'special snowflake' or laugh about the 'boo hoo generation' as a way of demeaning and undermining sensitivities that they have little ability of comprehending. It may look completely out of character. Here is a person you have come to know as being considerate and caring suddenly behaving in a strangely untypical fashion, but make no mistake, these are their real feelings breaking out. If this 'out of character' display is published online it will be a transitory appearance, often rapidly deleted when the narcissist realises just how much they have revealed about themselves.

When a narcissist discards a victim they are often happy to share that they were never attached to them and the lack of that person in their lives will not impact them at all. Not only did they not love you, they didn't even like you. You are dead to them. Listen when they say this. Don't try and imagine that they are just trying to hurt you and they don't really mean it. This is one of the few times when you can trust that they are actually speaking the truth. They do not have the capability to attach to other human beings in any meaningful way because this kind of intimacy terrifies them. Attachment requires a vulnerability that they are not able to tolerate.

A victim's response

Although narcissists use various techniques, the discard, when it comes, is often cowardly and rarely face to face. I've heard stories of relationships being ended via texts, emails or the narcissist simply disappearing. As painful as the discard may be, that might not be the end of the story. The narcissist likes to provoke their victims even after they have abandoned them. They will want to demonstrate how quickly they have moved on and how little their relationship meant to them. They really want their victim to feel pain. In a romantic relationship this will mean flaunting their new partner. In a family or friend situation this will most commonly be demonstrated by emphasising family get togethers with photos of happy faces posted publicly. This is our beautiful family and you don't belong. The narcissist doesn't want closure, they want you to feel confused and to leave an open wound they can sprinkle salt in whenever they feel the need.

The denial of closure may be heightened by them blocking and banning you from any and every communication channel immediately after the discard. They don't want to give you any opportunity to be able to respond to their accusations often because they are ridiculously trivial. The public view that they will present is that you are the abuser, they are the victim and they need to protect themselves from you.

A trait attributed to covert narcissists, particularly of the cerebral variety, is they think they have superior intelligence and can fool everyone. They often succeed, especially if they can take their time to write that considered and reasonable letter to the judge in a court case, or the lawyer when they're looking to sue an ex-friend for slander. However, social networking sites can be their undoing and it's possible to see the red flags flying high when they make comments or post statements that they haven't properly run through the covert thought editor.

You may see the covert narcissist boasting about how little they feel for the victim they have just discarded. This may well be couched in all the justifications as to why they have discarded their victim, which will be nothing to do with their actions, of course. All the same, in amongst the poor me, victim speak e.g., "I have put up with SO much over the years", will be the tell-tale signs of a disturbed personality. They mean nothing to me, never did and I've already moved on. Look for words like that in a public discard of a family member and you see the shadow of the covert narcissist peering out. Emotionally healthy people cannot turn love on and off. It's not a switch. When one is sifting through the bomb site left behind after the relationship has ended you can only come to the logical conclusion that they never had any feelings for you in the first place. You are correct. This may be the start of the scales falling from your eyes and the beginning of the healing process as you realise that a covert narcissist only has feelings for themselves. The bottom line is that they are the only person they truly care for. Over the years they will have realised that this is not publicly acceptable behaviour and have trained themselves to display family and romantic love to a degree. Scratch the surface though and inside they are an emotionally hollow shell. The person you loved never existed; you loved the person that the narcissist projected.

Although the narcissist closes off channels for discussion they still want to goad their victim. They are hoping for a reaction where you will let your guard down and they can use your angry response to justify the discard. Even a covert narcissist realises on some level that many people will not understand the discard of a close family member so they need hard evidence to prop up their decision. They do their best to taunt and goad in the hope that this will get a knee jerk reaction, the more extreme the better in their eyes. Your angry response will be displayed on their public social media page quicker than you can say copy and paste. See this is what we have to deal with, and people who have no idea of the real story will sympathise. The narcissist will get comments like, Wow you're amazing, I don't know how you have put up with it for so long, etc etc. This 'supply' will strengthen the narcissist's resolve to carry on with the goading under the guise of just posting family photos. Who could object to that?

If you have discovered that a family member is a narcissist you may have to face the loss of other family members if they are also in denial. The justifications and excuse making for a narcissist can be extraordinary and hard to stomach once you realise what you're dealing with. The level of dysfunction and intertwining of the narcissist and their enablers may be on such a level that no other members of the family will even consider what you're saying to have any credence, and you will be shunned for making such outrageous suggestions. You may find that the only way forward is breaking free and escaping from the narcissist and cutting off from your relatives in a similar fashion to a person who breaks free from a cult and has to leave their family behind. In the cult situation the behaviour is often similar. The escapee is shunned and a smear campaign often takes place where the community accuses the escapee of all sorts of 'crimes' and spreads the word that they are intrinsically a bad person. Given this explanation the rest of the community can feel justification for shunning the person who has got out because obviously they hadn't seen the light. Cult members can only feel pity and disgust for the person who has left.

We see this behaviour in other communities who close ranks, for example whistleblowers who expose poor practices in large organisations. They are often not hailed as heroes for pointing out dangerous failings but rather the organisation closes ranks and finds some spurious reason to counter accuse the whistleblower. Their credibility is lost often along with their job and status quo in the organisation is restored.

Similarly, in a dysfunctional family, when one member pulls the curtain back to reveal the narcissist for what they are, the rest of the family are likely to turn on the one who is revealing the problem. The public image of the family must be protected at all costs and the smear campaign will begin in earnest as the family closes in to protect its dysfunction from being revealed to the world. As this realisation dawns and the narcissist is aware that you have finally seen the real person behind the curtain they will act quickly. They need to devalue and discard you before you reveal them to others. At the instigation of the narcissist the family whistleblower will be called out on every 'sin' they have committed since the age of five. Listen for accusations that begin with "They were always…. 'They were never…" It is an attempt to self soothe in order that the rest of the family can feel that the shunning behaviour by the narcissist is justified. The scapegoat is bad and has always been inherently bad.

The inevitable estrangement must be explained with the narcissist adopting the role of victim. Within their own group of enablers the devaluation may have been happening for years, but now this is being spread to a wider audience.

As this process happens, your first reaction might be one of incredulity as you question what have you actually done to harm this person who is now carrying out a smear campaign against you.

Reacting to this onslaught of emotional abuse seems to be consistent with many of us. Confusion plays a large part initially. If you have suddenly had your eyes opened to the narcissistic behaviour of a family member that has been going on for many years, it is likely that you will be in shock.

Your whole relationship with that person may have been turned on its head. You may have believed you had a close, loving relationship when in fact it was a charade. It's likely that you were being mocked and belittled behind your back and the butt of family jokes. Any success of yours was greeted with derision and any failure cheered. You're reeling. How could you have been so stupid to have been taken in for so long? You may squirm in embarrassment as you think of all the times you have spoken proudly about the narcissist's successes. But then, as the narcissist begins to reveal anything they can to hurt you, the anger grows. They will sift through your past, like a detective at a crime scene, to find the most painful, traumatic and private incidents of your life and will then cruelly and casually share these in public in order to taunt you.

As an emotionally healthy adult the degree of anger that threatens to overwhelm you seems abnormal and you may wonder what is happening to you. Almost every person who is on the receiving end of this sort of behaviour has an enormous amount of rage. It is the beginning of the healing process. It can be enormously helpful to realise that it is a normal reaction to feel anger. When people who haven't been through it are telling you to get over it, calm down and are surprised at your strong reactions, they, with all the best intentions are minimising what's happened to you. It's important to know that the rage you feel is not abnormal and if you can channel it into something productive it can be helpful.

There are two points to remember. You have been hurt and in addition, to literally add insult to injury, the narcissist is now attempting to damage you in any way they can. Forgetting about it and moving on is excellent advice but for most of us, it is incredibly difficult to achieve when an important relationship has been proven to be a sham. Secondly, an angry reaction is exactly what the narcissist is relying on. They are goading you because they want you to react. They don't want you to quietly slip away, or people in their circle might start to doubt the narcissist's version of events. They need you to react and they will use any tactic to get a response from plain out lying about what you're supposed to have said or done, to making remarks about your children. Anything that they think will spark a reaction. No subject will be out of bounds.

It is a natural human instinct to defend ourselves when attacked and particularly if someone tell lies about us. We have a trigger, knee jerk response to give our side of the story and prove that what the narcissist is saying is wrong. As their stories get more extreme, outlandish and seemingly accepted without question by their group, we become more desperate to defend ourselves.

The problem is that once we start defending ourselves we are liable to make ourselves look guilty, and if we are not careful we'll be on the slippery slope to self destruction. We may become aggressive and there the narcissist has won. We have become what they said we were all along, the crazy person who is posting weird stuff on social media, all caps and screenshots. We have become obsessed, out of our minds with hurt, confusion, sadness and anger. We may start to suffer from depression and feel that nobody understands what we're going through. Of course if the narcissist finds out about this they won't feel sorry. Instead they will be experiencing a warm surge of satisfaction that they are now able to prove that they were right all along. You are suffering from mental health issues and are unstable. In the end, they will truly believe this version of events themselves, such is their ability for self delusion. To the world they will appear to be concerned for you, but in reality there is a celebration going on in their head. They have won again. Game, set and match.

You may feel the need to write out everything that has happened, to put the incidents in chronological order, to explain to the narcissist how they have hurt you in order to get some sort of closure. By all means write it out, journalling can really help to deal with the churning emotions when something like this occurs. However, if you write a letter to the narcissist I would urge you NOT to send it. It won't make any difference to how the narcissist feels except for making them happy as they now have 'proof' of your craziness or whatever else they want to 'prove' about you to their group. The likely outcome is that it will only cause more angst and heartache for you.

There may be a temptation to write about our experiences on social media platforms, calling out our abuser. For some reason we may be under the illusion that if it's written down nobody could doubt what we have gone through. In reality this kind of reaction, although perfectly understandable, is counter-productive. Friends or family who have never gone through this kind of experience will find it difficult to understand and are likely to think that you are overreacting.

The narcissist has honed their skills so that they will never be blamed for this situation. Why would a rant from you on social media make any difference? Again, you will just be proving their point. And if you think they will read your post and suddenly think, "Oh yes, I realise now. I AM a horrible person. It was my fault, I was totally in the wrong and I should apologise?" Of course that is never going to happen (unless of course they want to 'hoover' you in the future, but even then they are likely to be dismissive about what happened in the past rather than fake apologetic).

If you think you can educate their friends, or the wider world about their actions that is not likely to happen either. As we have seen they will have gathered their people around them, cut adrift anyone who might have challenged their behaviour and now have such a tight group that it will be all but impossible to make any impact on them.

Worse still, whatever you do will be spun to make you appear even more crazy. I'm sure we've all seen a furious rant, seemingly out of the blue, on our favourite social media site, taken a metaphorical step back and thought this person may be slightly disturbed to have such a reaction. Yep. However, these days, my first response to that situation is to assume that there is probably a covert narcissist somewhere in the background.

You may become obsessive for a while, wanting to talk about the situation and rehash every last sentence and nuance of the experience you've had with the narcissist. Again, this is a normal, natural reaction to having lived through such a surreal experience, when everything was turned on its head.

People who don't understand the way your emotions have been put through the wringer will almost certainly lose patience with the constant need to talk about it. That is where a support group can help. In a support group for survivors of narcissistic abuse you will find, sadly, thousands of people who have been through similar issues and will have an understanding of your need to talk and talk about what has happened to you. You can pour out your frustrations and vent your anger on a forum. You will get support and advice and in time you can learn to deal with the anger that threatens to overwhelm you. You can grieve for a lost relationship and in time you can move on.

One really important aspect of the 'after life' is not to react to anything the narcissist says. Ever. So what should we do? Ideally no-contact is the best method to deal with the narcissist. Cut off all contact, refuse to get hoovered back in, change your phone number and move if necessary. This is an extremely effective technique as it cuts off the fuel that keeps a narcissist's fire burning. With a friend or in a romantic relationship this tactic may be possible, you can move away, change jobs and never see or hear from the narcissist again if you're lucky. Although emotionally it may not be easy to sever all contact, at least in practical terms you may be able to distance yourself from the narcissist.

However, that may not be possible in practice, particularly if you are co-parenting or if the narcissist is a family member. There may be other family members that you want or need to keep in contact with and occasions such as weddings and funerals to consider. It may not be possible to cut the narcissist out of your life completely.

So the answer seems to be to remove yourself as much as possible from the situation and the next best technique seems to be to go 'grey rock' as mentioned earlier. This is a method of interacting with the narcissist but keeping all contact as low key as possible. Do not get into any animated conversation or argument with the narcissist but be as calm and boring as possible. Only indulge in superficial conversations, don't get sucked into anything that could be controversial. It is likely that the narcissist will try and provoke you but the key here is to offer monosyllabic answers and not to bite at the provocation. This approach will starve the narcissist of supply and after the initial confusion they are likely to get bored and try elsewhere.

It is also a technique that can be practised as an adult child with a narcissistic parent. If you feel tense on a visit 'home' you can make it into a private game, mentally scoring yourself for all the times that you didn't bite when the prov-ocation was laid down before you. Now you can see how the narcissist is trying to manipulate you, it can be a lot easier to respond in a more positive way. If it's possible, always take someone else with you. The narcissist will not be able to be overtly provocative if they are trying to maintain their 'public' image in front of, for example, a partner. However, they will know exactly how to press your buttons. A look, or even a smile at the 'wrong' time has the potential to take you back to being a small child again and your instinct will be to react. If you don't react, score yourself bonus points and smile back.

You can control this situation now, they can throw down all the provocation they like but they cannot control how you react to it. Like anything, the more you practice this approach the more adept you will become. The narcissist will be confused and frustrated and may eventually stop trying to push your buttons. You may find this is the time you can reestablish a relationship but this time on your terms, as an equal. If you can separate yourself from the past, progress can be made. I'm not advocating 'forgive and forget', but I am saying if this is someone that you feel the need to stay in contact with it has the potential to be a way of coping with what can otherwise be a re-traumatising situation.

In many ways, the experience of discovering that a relationship you cherished was based on a narcissistic lie can be enriching. I know that seems a contradictory statement but in my own experience it has opened my eyes and I began to see how other people were manipulating or being manipulated. It helped me with my own non-narcissistic relationships to question motives for my actions. You may even look back on past relationships and have that 'aha' moment when you realise that the person you dated thirty years ago, who disappeared for two weeks and then reappeared complete with a rich and detailed story about being hunted by gangland murderers was almost certainly a narcissist and was almost certainly lying.

An important caveat here is that these techniques of no-contact and grey rock will not work on all narcissists. The malignant, violent narcissist may become enraged if you employ these coping mechanisms and they see their control slipping away.

Conclusion

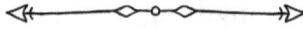

I t can be shocking to discover that a friend or a family member has a personality disorder that falls within the Narcissistic Personality Disorder spectrum. You may feel that your whole life has been turned upside down as you delve deeper into the psyche of the disordered person's world. It can be disturbing to read narcissistic abuse survivor forums with contributors writing about the similar circumstances. It's almost as if they had lived with your narcissist, the conversations and incidents are so similar to your own experience. It can be a surreal moment when you realise that this is not just your own problem but is a recognised condition and it's not YOU losing your mind or being a terrible person for finally challenging the narcissist. It is as if someone has drawn back a curtain and you see the reality for the first time, maybe in decades. You suddenly realise how you have been shut down and silenced.

As you look back over your past relationship with your abuser, the confusion begins to make sense. The tantrums and controlling behaviour that led to you walk on eggshells to avoid confrontation. The strange shame they exhibited when one of their children didn't 'live up to their expectations'. The cutting off of almost their whole family at different times during their life, the discarding and hoovering. The constant drama that surrounded their life and family.

You are likely to have 'aha' moments at unexpected times, triggered by anything and everything as you remember an incident and realise now that it was narcissistic behaviour.

The more you educate yourself about these disorders the more you give yourself power and permission to see what has really happened within this relationship and how you have been manipulated. If you have someone who is supporting you through this crisis you may find yourself starting sentences with "OMG do you remember that time when they (insert strange behaviour here)", as you recall an incident which is now, in hindsight, a typical narcissistic red flag.

From a personal point of view, after the hurt and upset caused by the final discard there came a sense of relief when I realised that I no longer had to tolerate this confusing behaviour and the stress ebbed away. It appears to be fairly common that, within lengthy family relationships, you don't even recognise the build up of stress until after the discard. Then the sense of relief can be overwhelming. Likewise, you won't even have realised that you were in an abusive relationship. Traditionally, we are taught that abusive relationships are all about violence, at the least shouting and screaming but for many of us who have had contact with a covert narcissist it is much more subtle and hard to pin down.

After the discard I felt stupid not to have seen this. I had defended and made excuses for my abuser, I wouldn't hear a word said against them and would take on all comers to defend them. I was in denial in the biggest way possible and couldn't see what they were doing even though I was more than capable of analysing other's behaviours. I realise now that I carried around with me an uncomfortable sense of having to be careful about what I said. The slight nagging doubt about our relationship could never be articulated and I buried it deep. I shrugged it off as my imaginings. As they pulled away I made more and more extreme excuses even though the damning evidence of their lies and avoidance was right in front of my eyes. I refused to see it until they properly initiated the devalue and discard phase.

Even after the discard I had no language for what had happened. It wasn't until I began researching borderline personality disorder for another project that the penny finally dropped. BPD has some crossover with Narcissistic Personality Disorder and striking similarities began to jump out at me. I recognised red flags and signs that this is what had happened to me and perfectly described my abuser. The more I educated myself, the more I realised that this was a classic case and all the signs were there for anyone to see. Except me, at the time.

However, along with all the negatives, the whole experience has enriched my life. That might be strange to say but the final devalue and discard has freed me from a damaging relationship and the uncomfortable feeling of something being wrong but never being able to put my finger on it. The more I've learned about narcissism the more I've been able to see patterns emerging and interestingly it has revealed behaviours going back generations. It has taken away much of the despair and condemnation that I felt initially. I now only feel pity for the damage they have done to some of the most valuable relationships of their life, and sympathy for the emptiness they feel inside, and the desperation that drives them to fill that up in whatever way he can.

However, this is not the kind of sympathy that allows me to be pulled back into a relationship with an abuser but one that can build understanding. A narcissist's life is miserable, full of jealousy and hate. They are constantly on alert for any slight they can become enraged about. They become 'grievance gatherers' collecting lists of how they have been wronged. They spend many hours living out revenge fantasies in their head. The only time they are genuinely happy is if they're 'getting one over' on their 'enemy'. The older they get the worse this becomes as they make more enemies in the people that surround them in real life. At the same time they have the pressure of maintaining the 'perfect' social media facade so that their 'friends', who consist mostly of people who don't know them personally never find out who they truly are. They have very few 'real life' friends who still tolerate them. They become bitter and push the people who once loved them away. They are paranoid that people are plotting and planning against them because that is how they spend their own days. Their hate campaigns take over their lives and it's all they can talk about. The pressure of such an existence can only lead to unbearable stress.

We all have some narcissistic traits, it is part of life and a survival mechanism. Recognising how and when that transforms into a disorder and becomes problematic is an important skill to acquire. In schools currently we are teaching young people about abusive relationships and that it's not okay to stay with someone who hits you or bullies you. If schools could teach about the subtleties of love-bombing, gaslighting and triangulation this would be an invaluable life lesson and allow young people to recognise potentially abusive relationships from the outset.

In parallel with writing this book I've been researching religious cults. Even at a cursory level many comparable conclusions can be drawn between narcissism and cults specifically some of the practices such as 'disconnection' and 'fair game' in the Church of Scientology and 'shunning' and theocratic war strategy in the Jehovah's Witness.

Disconnection and shunning are policies in Scientology and Jehovah's Witnesses respectively that actively discourage communication with people who have become enemies of the church. This enemy status leads to becoming a 'suppressive person' in the case of Scientology and being 'disfellowshipped' in the case of Jehovah's Witnesses. Fair game is a policy that anyone deemed to be a 'suppressive person' ie an enemy of the Church of Scientology, may be tricked, sued or lied to or destroyed. The policy was officially scrapped years ago but appears to have survived, albeit in an unauthorised capacity. Theocratic war is a device used by Jehovah's Witnesses to justify lying. According to the JW publication 'Aid to Bible Understanding', "Lying generally involves saying something false to a person who is entitled to know the truth..." If you are critical of the organisation or even just a 'worldly' person and not a Jehovah's Witness you may not be entitled to the truth and can legitimately, in the eyes of the Watchtower organisation, be lied to.

Friends and family members, in both organisations, are strongly encouraged not to have anything to do with the disconnected or disfellowshipped. This leads to shunning of parents by children and vice versa. Rather than engaging in conversation people are shut down and excluded, lies are told, smear campaigns are begun...

The more I research the behaviour of cults; the lying, the indoctrination, brainwashing, the devaluing, discarding and shunning, the more narcissism and the narcissistic family in particular resembles a mini cult. A powerful reminder to distance ourselves from damaging groups!

Onward and upward

For all that these relationships can be devastating, the part where we begin to educate ourselves about the condition and share our experiences with others is when we begin to understand the reality. This is not us 'losing our minds', it really did happen, and it's not even that unusual.

Allow yourself some time to recover. This is not insignificant. When you're feeling so angry you can't sleep and you need to analyse the actions of the narcissist over and over be assured that this is a perfectly normal reaction. When friends or family advise you to 'get over it' and 'move on', no matter how kindly it is meant, they are likely to have no idea of the damage this kind of relationship can have. Complex Post-Traumatic Stress Disorder (C-PTSD) can develop in the aftermath of a narcissistic abusive relationship. It's beyond the scope of this book to examine the details of the psychological issues arising from these relationships, but I would urge you to research and as mentioned previously get support from people who understand what you're going through.

Due to the fast moving nature of the internet instead of listing resources for support I would encourage you to search the web for "narcissistic abuse support". Join several support forums to find the best fit for you.

I hope this book has been helpful in some way and I can only reiterate that confronting a narcissist, especially a covert narcissist can be dangerous. Once the mask has been pulled away they no longer have much left to lose.

Please do not put your life in danger, keep safe and get some support.

Bibliography

Joanna Kujath. Conversation With A Narcissist: 12 Things To Look Out For. 2017. YouTube, https://www.youtube.com/watch?v=UC09nTGKOEo.

'Narcissistic Personality Disorder - Symptoms and Causes'. Mayo Clinic. Accessed 24 July 2018. http://www.mayoclinic.org/diseases-conditions/narcissistic-personality-disorder/symptoms-causes/syc-20366662.

Wikipedia contributors, "Narcissistic rage and narcissistic injury," Wikipedia, The Free Encyclopedia, https://en.wikipedia.org/w/index.php?title=Narcissistic_rage_and_narcissistic_injury&oldid=844835016

psychologytoday.com

thoughtcatalog.com

thriveafterabuse.com

Dana Morningstar
facebook.com/pg/ThriveAfterAbuse/videos/

Richard Grannon
youtube.com/user/SPARTANLIFECOACH

Harefield Press

More books by this author

ART

Dog Days

61 Rabbits

HISTORY

Walks Thru' Coventry

Chasing Rainbows

CHILDREN'S PICTURE BOOK

Too Big for Bunnies

harefieldpress.com

amazon.com/author/paulajeffery